COPYWRITING FOR PODCASTERS

COPYWRITING FOR
PODCASTERS

How to *Grow* Your PODCAST, BRAND, and BUSINESS with *Compelling Copy*

Laura Petersen
M.A.E.D.

Author:

Laura Petersen, M.A.E.D.

Title:

Copywriting for Podcasters: How to Grow Your Podcast, Brand, and Business with Compelling Copy

Series:

This book is the first in a series by Laura Petersen.

Subjects:

Podcasting, Writing Tips, Storytelling, Psychology, Online Marketing, Networking, Media Exposure, Adult Education.

Rights:

First Edition
ISBN-13: 978-1540854889
ISBN-10: 1540854884

Disclaimer:

Although the author and publisher have made every effort to ensure that the information in this book was correct at press time, the author and publisher do not assume and hereby disclaim any liability to any party for any loss, damage, or disruption caused by errors or omissions, whether such errors or omissions result from negligence, accident, or any other cause.

Cover Illustration Copyright © 2016 Laura Petersen

Cover Design by Olena Beley

Editing by Emily Hickok

Foreword by Brandon T. Adams

Chapter Illustrations © 2016 Laura Petersen

Thank you to contributing industry influencers [in alphabetical order]:

Adrian Aguilar
Amanda Bond
Andrew Steven
Bernard Paraiso
Brandon T. Adams
Elsie Escobar
Jared Easley
Jay Wong
Jessica Kupferman
Jessica Rhodes
Jill Stanton
John Lee Dumas
Khierstyn Ross
Marcus Meurer
Melissa Sue Tucker
Michael O'Neal
Stephen Christopher
Stephen Dela Cruz
Yaro Starak

This book would not have come about without the collaborations, teachings, and support of Dominick Sirianni (my partner at Podtent Marketing[1]) and Melissa Sue Tucker (my partner at Podcast Teachers[2]).

Special thanks to Brandon T. Adams, Eric Yang, James Altucher, and Dan Tieman for your advice and encouragement to put my teachings into book form.

And, of course, a huge thank you to my husband, Devin Shepard, for putting up with my work addiction and supporting me through the years of long hours.

I guess that's what happens when you finally love what you do. And we entrepreneurs are the only people who will work 80+ hours a week to avoid the 40-hour work week.

Lastly, this book is dedicated to every entrepreneur who wants to grow his or her brand and business through the power of podcasting and content marketing.

It all ties together and it is my intention to help you put the pieces together for more success.

---

[1] http://podtentmarketing.com/
[2] http://podcastteachers.com/

Welcome!

A Free Gift to My Readers:

Get free, instant access to all the tools and extras I mention in this book that I could not fit in. Examples include:

- Links to videos and articles mentioned throughout the book
- My Podcast Intros & Outros Chart [fillable]
- My Shownotes Template [fillable]
- Transcription Services I recommend
- 9 Important Sound Tips for Podcast Hosts and Guests
- Links to Free and Paid Resources to Find Podcast Guests
- And more

To help you implement what you learn in this book, I have made these tools available online, which you can access here: www.PodcastTeachers.com/book-freebies[3]

UPDATE:

Additionally, I have gotten such a great response from this book, and the process of writing it and hitting #1 best-seller on Amazon in both the United States and Canada the day that I launched, that I have started helping others get the same or BETTER results with a business book in their niche.

Visit **CopyThatPops.com/free-training** for more.

What You Will Get from This Book:

Laura Petersen is a Math and Psychology teacher turned "digital nomad" entrepreneur who took lessons learned from growing a tutoring and test prep company to the world of podcasting and content marketing.

She holds a Bachelor's degree in Psychology with a minor in German after graduating *magna cum laude* from UCLA, a Master's in Education *with honors*, and a Teaching English as a Foreign Language Certificate.

Her popular podcast Copy That Pops[4] analyzes how to leverage effective copywriting tips and Psychology hacks for better results in your business.

After writing and editing more pages than possible to count for her own businesses and her clients, interviewing experts from different industries, and testing strategies in her own projects, Laura brings together lessons learned to show you exactly how to improve the writing that permeates every aspect of your podcast to grow it, your brand, and, ultimately, your business.

In this book, Laura will break concepts down and show you how they tie together, putting compelling copy to work toward achieving your goals.

She also includes:

- examples so you can SEE concepts in action in real life

---

[4] http:// copythatpops.com/podcast

- (fun) pop quizzes to check your understanding
- advice and insights from other influencers in podcasting and online business
- activities for you to try so that you can implement new learning immediately

That is the best way to improve and grow.

Apply it immediately.

To continue the conversation around podcasting and how to grow your podcast, brand, and business, please connect with Laura on Facebook, Instagram, or Twitter @LaptopLaura.

To learn more about her work helping other entrepreneurs become best-selling authors and leveraging it to grow their industry authority, media exposure, and business, visit Copy That Pops[5].

After growing your podcast, the next best step is to become a published author. Hitting #1 in Amazon is another goal to add to that, which is achievable with the right approach.

In This Book You Will Learn

Laura's 15 favorite ways to leverage writing for growing your podcast, brand, and business including:

1. Storytelling (throughout everything)
2. Show-Stopping Shownames
3. Not-So-Subtle Subtitles
4. iTunes Podcast Show Descriptions

---

5 https://www.copythatpops.com/

Contents

PART 3: REAP YOUR HARVEST

Foreword

by Brandon T. Adams

Orlando, Florida

November 26, 2016

THE FIRST TIME I talked with Laura Petersen was on October 10, 2016, just 47 days ago.

In that short time span, she has blown me away with her writing, podcast production skills, and entrepreneurial drive and acumen.

We met because of a Mastermind Accelerator program[6] that I launched to help other entrepreneurs take their business and lifestyle to a whole new level.

I may still be just 26 years old, but I've accomplished a lot and have many lessons to share.

Here are a few of the tenants that you will always hear me teach and preach:

1. You are the average of the people you spend the most time with.
2. Get visibility and earn celebrity status in your niche.
3. Add value always -- even for free -- to work with high-profile influencers.

---

[6] http://LivetoGrind.com/influencer

1. You are the average of the people you spend the most time with.

In that very first Skype call with Laura, I told her about how the Influencer Mastermind was designed to help everyone to increase their 'average.'

Masterminds are so important, and ones that are pay-to-join attract business people with more skin in the game, looking to make bigger moves.

I myself did the School of Greatness with Lewis Howes and got more than my money's worth of returned value by building a relationship with Lewis and collaborating with others in the group.

If you are not in a mastermind[7] yet, find one immediately.

2. Get visibility and earn celebrity status in your niche.

This is where I really shine. I am not afraid of the microphone or camera!

With the cover of Inventors Digest, three podcasts, a reality T.V. show going into Season 2, and a love for Snapchat and Facebook Live, not a day passes without my hopping into the public eye to share my message. I have even appeared on news programs all over the country, Grant Cardone TV, NBC, and USA Today.

Therefore, I encouraged Laura to find ways to get more visible.

Make a bigger splash.

---

[7] http://LivetoGrind.com/influencer

This book is a huge step in the right direction, and I applaud her for setting the goal to write a book and hit Amazon Best Seller in just 1 month.

And she did it!

With content that is second to none.

That's hustle *and* skill combined.

3. Add value always -- even for free -- to work with high-profile influencers.

For me, I have had the honor of running crowdfunding campaigns, earning over $1 million in just 12 months for the likes of John Lee Dumas and the film *THINK: The Legacy of Think and Grow Rich*.

I am also collaborating with Kevin Harrington, an original shark from ABC's Shark Tank, and have upcoming projects with Forbes Riley and others.

I guess this is why they call me the "King of Crowdfunding."

So, I gave Laura the homework assignment early on in the mastermind to list out 5 influencers she would want to do work for — for free — just to build a relationship with them.

Her company Podtent Marketing does high-touch, done-for-you podcast launch and content marketing production services, so I knew she had a lot to offer.

When the assignment came due, Laura listed out 5 influencers and then threw one more into the mix.

Me!

I was simultaneously surprised and excited, because I had started to see the level of detail and quality she even put into her email responses to my questions.

For nearly 4 weeks now, Laura has been editing my Live to Grind podcasts (twice a week), writing up incredibly detailed shownotes that are boosting my SEO, creating social media share images to promote each episode, and helping me turn out even more content inspired by the episodes.

Talk about creating value.

Laura is now completely managing my podcast as the official Executive Producer and we are planning big things for 2017.

So, let's turn to this book.

I believe that podcasting is one of the best ways to connect with a new audience, build relationships with influencers, and gain massive industry credibility.

If you have a podcast already, or are thinking of starting one, good.

Dive in fully.

It is through podcasting that I got to connect with John Lee Dumas and go on to help him raise nearly $500,000 for The Freedom Journal.

Use this book to help craft compelling copy that both gets you found by search engines and turns visitors into listeners and customers.

Laura is a thought leader in the space of podcasting.

And with a background in teaching, psychology, and copywriting, she has the ultimate trifecta to help you grow your podcast, brand, and business with awesome writing.

She really lays it all out for you in this book.

And the internationally notable influencers she reached out to contribute even more to what you are about to read. Nowhere else will you find their insights on where copywriting and podcasting converge for business success.

I am confident you will get a lot of value from the contents of these chapters. Just as I have from all my interactions with Laura.

Happy podcasting and writing,

Brandon T. Adams

CEO & Founder
Live to Grind
Accelerant   Media Group
Arctic Stick
Accelerant Magazine

**T.V. Co-Host &
Executive Producer**
Ambitious Adventures
Live to Grind T.V.

PART 1:
PLANTING THE SEEDS

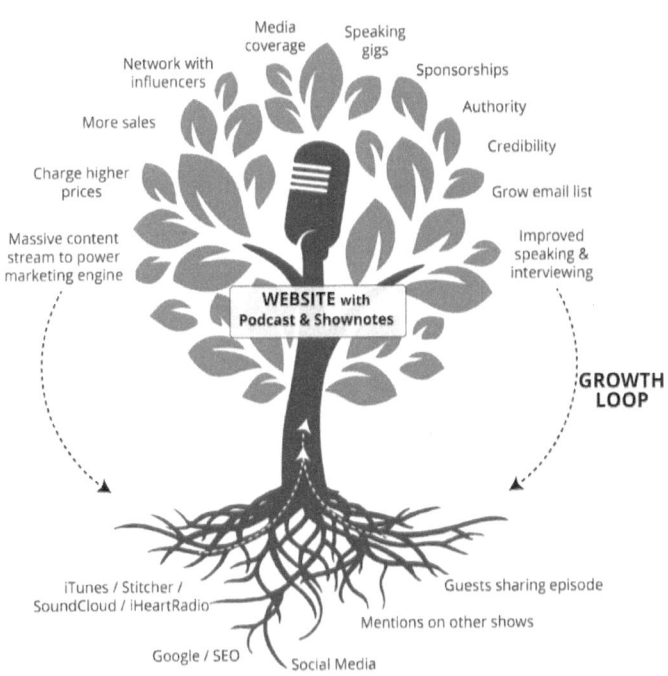

1.1: 15 Benefits of Podcasting for Brand and Business Growth

BEFORE WE EVEN TALK about how to grow your podcast -- whether you have one already or are preparing to launch your own -- let's talk about why it's freaking smart to have one.

Here are just a few of the benefits podcasting entrepreneurs can realize as they grow their podcast, brand, and business:

1. Exposure to new audiences (e.g. iTunes, Stitcher, SoundCloud, iHeartRadio, GooglePlay, Apple CarPlay)
2. Ability to more deeply connect and communicate with your audience
3. Increased credibility
4. Improved industry authority
5. Stronger networking with influencers (starting a conversation with "I'd love to put you in front of my audience" sure beats the dreaded "Can I pick your brain over coffee?")
6. Media coverage (other podcasts, news articles, T.V., etc.)

7. Lots of great, original content (for your inbound marketing efforts)
8. Improved SEO and more web traffic
9. Increased social shares and engagement
10. Email list growth
11. Better speaking and interviewing skills
12. Increased sales of your products and services
13. Ability to charge more for your products and services
14. Sponsorships
15. Paid speaking opportunities

And the great thing about these benefits is that they are in a growth loop. As one increases, it leads to others increasing too, in a continuous spiral upward!

1.2: Visualizing a Podcast's Role in the Business Success Ecosystem

HALFWAY THROUGH WRITING THIS book I woke up one Saturday morning and an idea struck me!

Podcasts play an important role in the success of growing a business. But how can I SHOW people instead of just TELLing them?

I opened up a little notebook I have on my desk (that I got from the Thrive conference in San Diego from the folks at Thinkific) for great ideas pertaining to writing this book and started to draw out some thoughts.

For those of you who know me, my husband is a Horticulturalist, so plants are discussed often in my household, even if I'd rather be talking about new social media hacks.

Eventually my scribbles turned into a recognizable form.

A tree.

With deep roots, a solid trunk, and lots of leaves.

Here's my original sketch here from 11/12/16 about 6:30 am.

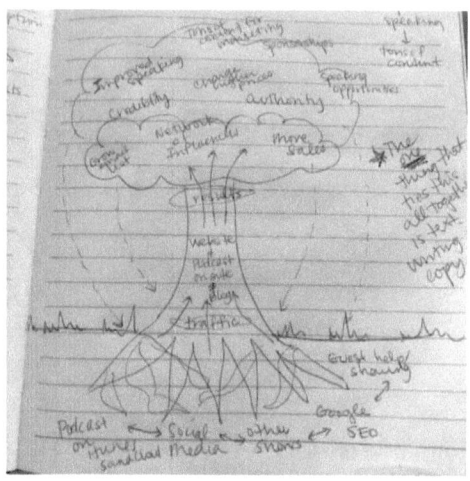

This drawing, this idea, helped me capture how it all comes together.

You see, a podcast is a tool. It's a GREAT tool to grow brand recognition and all the other monikers of success as an entrepreneur.

But how you grow your podcast does not stand in isolation from the rest of your business. They are a part of the same complex system.

And like a tree, the fruits of your labor do not appear overnight. You need to water it, give it fresh air, sunlight, and time to grow.

But if you do things correctly and intentionally, it will grow. It will produce fruit.

After some back and forth with a few designers on Fiverr.com and adding the text myself using Adobe Illustrator, I had my final tree!

Here it is again (also pictured at the beginning of this section).

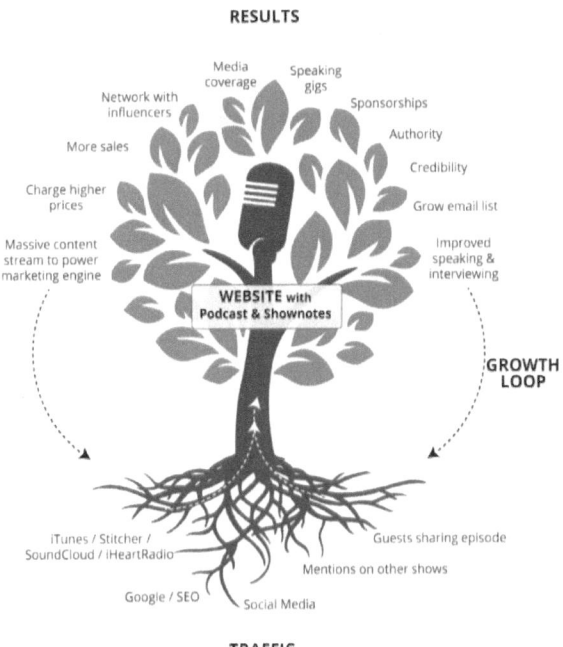

Having a podcast is a terrific tool to generate more traffic from audio playing platforms like iTunes, search engines like Google, and social media shares all over.

That traffic drives to the central core of your business, your website. On your site, you have the podcast embedded along with shownotes, and, most importantly, opportunities for the traffic to engage with you further and convert into email subscribers, leads, customers, and raving fans.

That extra traffic and growth, combined with other benefits of podcasting, leads to further results (shown in the leaves of the tree) such as sponsorships, speaking gigs, and traditional media coverage.

These desirable results trickle back down to the roots and feed the tree even further.

But one thing that is vital to note here is...

[Continue to the next chapter to find out!]

1.3: The One Common Denominator

AS I DREW THE tree in detail with roots, the trunk, and leaves, I realized that the ONE thing that is constant, the ONE thing that ties it all together in this ecosystem is the written word.

Text.

Copy.

Writing.

Copywriting.

No podcasting entrepreneur who wants to be successful can escape writing.

Google cannot find you from just your audio.

iTunes does not rank your show just by how highly produced your intro and outro are.

And big name guests are not going to just appear out of thin air early on.

You need to leverage the power of effective and compelling copy to get all you want out of your podcast.

...But don't stress if you don't feel like an awesome writer just yet. That is what this book is for. Keep going!

1.4: Why Writing's Hard But You Have to Do It Well Anyway

HAVE YOU NOTICED HOW preschoolers suck at writing?

Imagine asking a 4-year old to write a few sentences about why she wants to go to Disneyland and you are likely to get garbled pseudo-letters and a few indiscernible cartoon character drawings.

Oh, but ask her to TELL you why she wants to go to Disneyland!

Now I'll bet you that she even gets the grouchiest of adults to smile and feel compelled to help get her to her dream destination.

[I actually say I cannot be dragged to Disneyland -- to the shock of many -- but if my nieces were to ask with excitement in their voices, I'd be convinced quite quickly, I am sure. Just don't tell them that.]

What's the point of this comparison?

The fact of the matter is that we humans have been speaking for far longer than we have been writing. Scientists estimate language began about 100,000 years ago, but we have only seen writing for about 5,216 years (at the time of composing this book, at least ;)).

We have been speaking for about 95,000 years *longer* than we have been writing.

Our own childhood development follows this pattern as well. We all speak long before we can write. [Thus why the average preschooler can get her point across with speaking but not writing].

So, it is only natural that most of us are far better at speaking than we are at writing. Many of you may have been drawn to podcasting for this very reason.

- You love talking to people.
- You love the creative brainstorming aloud that comes from a great conversation.
- You recognize that content is vital to business these days. But it's a lot easier to record a conversation than it is to stare at a blank screen and force yourself to write blog articles.
- You are able to convey your personality, energy, passion, and wisdom more quickly and easily through speaking.
- Hearing your voice adds an extra layer of rapport that can be built with your audience and target market beyond words on a page.

But...there's a catch.

The search engine algorithms of our day cannot quantify how relevant and high-quality your podcast episodes are without text to "crawl."

The algorithms hungrily search out titles, descriptions, shownotes, social media posts, and more before they deem your content worthy of showering you with the traffic that you so desperately need to grow and thrive.

And to harvest all the fruits of your labor.

What's more, most internet users still engage via reading content. [Despite how much video and audio are growing.]

Visitors will give you a few seconds worth of a chance to grab them with your headlines, tweets, and bulleted lists, but bore them and they're gone.

Confuse them, and they'll bounce.

It turns out that even podcasters need to be good at writing.

Even podcasters need a few copywriting strategies and hacks in their arsenal to get all they want from their podcast, brand, and business.

1.5: Who Is This Book For?

I'VE WRITTEN THIS BOOK with a few groups of people in mind.

1. Any entrepreneur who wants to launch a podcast soon.

My motto is all about applying as you learn. So if you are going to start a podcast soon, terrific!

You found this book at the perfect time!

Go through each chapter, step-by-step, and craft your perfect copy so that you launch your podcast with the best foot forward.

2. Any entrepreneur who has a podcast already and wants to improve it, its growth, and its impact on their entire brand and business.

Have you ever wanted to get more downloads and generate more leads from your podcast, but feel like you've tried everything and it's just not getting the exposure it should?

You have a great show, interesting guests, and you've worked hard (investing time and maybe a bit of money) into intro music, a microphone, and software to help you produce a great show. You may have even hired a virtual assistant to help delegate some of the tedious tasks.

But those downloads just aren't climbing like you'd hope.

More downloads = bigger audience = more engagement and more conversions of sales of your product or service = more industry authority = more attention = more downloads.

So what gives?

It's your writing.

"But no!" you shout.

"I started a podcast because I love talking and listening. It's more engaging than writing and easier to create great content."

True, true. I feel you.

But here's the thing... the current technology of search engines relies on robots crawling through text. To be found, you still need strategically crafted words.

And although podcasts are on the rise, many people first come across you and your business through your blog, your Facebook posts or ads, or by reading the description of your show on iTunes.

It takes extra effort for a visitor to decide to become a listener.

And then more effort to turn a listener into a customer and raving fan.

So you have to have killer copy. Compelling communication in the written word.

3. Entrepreneurs without a podcast, who may consider it.

People who want to see more of what goes into crafting the messaging all around a great podcast to see if podcasting can fit well into their business (spoiler alert: it can) can also benefit from what we discuss in this book.

And get this:

Compelling copywriting advice actually applies to all entrepreneurs, whether you have a podcast or not. After all, podcasts fit so snugly into the full business ecosystem!

This book is also for you if you:

Can write but you don't think you're that great at it [or at least you are not sure how to apply your writing skills to the podcasting world].

- Are pressed for time and need examples to see what to aim for.

- Have an amazing service or problem-solving products that truly help your clients. You want to optimize the marketing channel that is your podcast to get more industry authority, credibility, sales, and increase your network and circle of influence.

- Realize that the "dream podcast guests" you want to interview in your space will judge you on more than one factor when deciding to say yes or no for an interview.

  The way you communicate in writing with them via email, on social media, and by the description you have on your podcast weighs heavily on their decision. If it's not professional and polished, they will not want to associate themselves with it or you.

- Know people care about 'proof of success' like download numbers and others sharing and engaging with your content.

- Feel overwhelmed by all you need to work on and want guidance at an affordable price. You are not ready for a done-for-you copywriting service.

1.6: What's in This Book?

I'VE COMPILED TOP-NOTCH, compelling copywriting tips, strategies, and templates from both my own experience and from successful online business and podcasting influencers around the globe.

You will find all the juicy details in Part 2 of this book.

We look at elements of compelling copy and how to apply them to the different areas around your podcast and beyond that to support impactful growth of your brand and business a whole.

Remember, the podcast does not stand in isolation.

For clarity, each chapter follows this general pattern

1. What is it?
2. Why should podcasters care? Benefits to your brand and business
3. Laura's experience
4. Great examples
5. Insights from an influencer

6. How to implement this right now

7. Pop Quiz

Make sure to do the activities and quizzes in each chapter to start applying what you learn right away.

Take it from me (a teacher :))! That is the best way to get the most out of this book and start seeing results in your own podcast, brand, and business.

1.7: My Story

SO WHO THE HECK am I? Here's a chronology.

My background:

The 90's:

- Self-proclaimed nerd in school. I took all the Advanced Placement (A.P.) and Honors classes I could. And I used to race my bestie (and book editor) Emily Hickok on listing all the presidents in order the fastest. You know, nerd stuff.
- I thought getting good grades, going to the best college possible, and then getting a great job (like a Psychology professor at an elite university) was the only path for me.
- Oh, and I was #23 on the basketball team. Go, Jordan!

2001-2002:

- Studied abroad in Germany for a year, as a junior.

2002:

- Returned home depressed -- after the best year of my life -- only wanting to travel more although I had no money and missed my new friends terribly.

- My dad gave me the book *Rich Dad, Poor Dad* by Robert Kiyosaki. That, plus my new travel obsession, changed the course of my life forever.

2003:

- Graduated early from U.C.L.A. with a Bachelor's degree in Psychology, minor in German, and with *magna cum laude* honors to start helping a realtor in my hometown so that I could learn about Real Estate and start investing like Robert taught.
PS: Hi, Ruthie Truscott! Thanks for everything. :)
- Realized that starting a Real Estate business was a lot of hard work and I'd need to set up shop in one place pretty much forever (referrals are the best in that business) but didn't want to spend my entire life in Orange County, California and didn't want client calls every night and through the weekends, so I moved to Arizona where houses were cheaper and it felt different.

2005:

- Bought a house, watched it tick up for a few months, and then completely bottom out and sit "underwater" for about 9 years.

2005-2007:

- Tried starting some businesses that didn't work out.
- Was shocked to find out that no one wanted to pay me what I *thought* I was worth (a

degree in Psychology, even from UCLA was surprisingly not as valuable as I was lead to believe ;)) and ran back to what I knew best: Education.

- Earned a Master's in Secondary Education and teaching credential, opting to knock it out fast and stay in Arizona rather than head to Ph.D. programs in Psychology (to which I was accepted by several school) elsewhere in the U.S.

2006-2011:

- Taught Honors Math and A.P. Psychology at a high school for about 5 years.
- Traveled abroad every second we had a school break. I got to explore Peru, Southeast Asia, Europe multiple times, Mexico, Belize, Guatemala, Costa Rica, and more.
- Learned the importance of clarity in writing to avoid 150 questions from teenage students like, "What's on the exam?" or "When is this due?"

2011 - present:

- 'Retired' from teaching full-time just as I was turning 30 and made the leap to entrepreneurism. It was a burning desire that never quite.
- Started a tutoring and test prep company called Student-Tutor with a business partner (Todd Van Duzer).
- We grew our blog with great content to 65,000+ sessions a month.

- Created and taught courses on SAT prep and ACT prep.
- Hired, trained, and coached tutors and staff so that now it runs without my daily invention. So thankful for them all.
- Learned so many lessons on business.

2013 - 2014:

- Adopted our dog Tuck (10 pounds, never-barks, minpin-chihuahua) from a rescue shelter.
- Was asked by Dominick Sirianni, the creator and host of the Internet Marketing Association's podcast IMA Leader to help with content and promotion. I'd listen to each episode, write up detailed shownotes, compose catchy tweetables and images, and share them all over the social platforms. I also wrote blog articles inspired by the guests.
- Was asked by a large media company to do social media and content writing for them and their clients too.
- Other notables: Got married, honeymooned in Panama, and moved to downtown San Diego.

2015:

- **October:**
  - After a year in San Diego, moved to Europe with my husband and Tuck for an adventure.
  - Completed a Teaching English as a Foreign Language (TEFL) certification course in Prague (for fun), then rented an

apartment in Regensburg, Germany where we took German lessons and explored the region until the weather warmed up.

- **December:**
  - o Dominick Sirianni contacted me while I was in Germany with the idea for Podtent Marketing[8]. A done-for-you service for mid-sized companies to launch their podcast and use it at the forefront of a content marketing strategy.

2016:

- **February:**
  - o We started getting our first clients just from being active in Facebook groups (thanks Bryan Harris' Rapid List Building course!) and the strong networks we have both been building for years.
- **April:**
  - o Started my own podcast called Copy That Pops[9] around my nerdy interests of copywriting, Psychology, and entrepreneurism as we traveled from Germany to Greece, Italy, Ireland, and back to the U.S.
- **Summer:**
  - o We went to Croatia for my birthday, I attended a 10-day Digital Nomad retreat in Greece, then we lived in Rome for 5 weeks and Ireland for 3 weeks. Add in trips to Spain and Austria (I swear there is

---

[8] http://podtentmarketing.com/
[9] http://copythatpops.com/podcast

a town there called Fucking -- I have pics to prove it).

- **August:**
    - o We decided to return home to the States after just the year of excitement we needed, feeling refreshed and more motivated than ever.
- **Early October:**
    - o Started Podcast Teachers[10] with my mastermind buddy Melissa Sue Tucker, who I met in a Facebook group also while in Germany, to help entrepreneurs start their own podcast to grow their brand and business (even if they can't afford a done-for-you full service).
    - o Our Mission: Help 1,000 entrepreneurs launch their own podcast that grows their business and brand by 12/31/17.
- **Late October:**
    - o Joined Brandon T. Adams's first Influencer Mastermind Accelerator[11] and attended *Thrive: Make Money Matter* in San Diego, where we relocated back to after our year in Europe.
    - o In the span of 1 week, three people I consider mentors (personally or from afar) told me to write a book.
    - o After seeing my insanely detailed and thoughtful, yet organized and clear emails and shownotes, Brandon insisted that I write a book. #duh Sometimes you need a mentor to point out the obvious.

---

[10] http://podcastteachers.com/
[11] http://livetogrind.com/influencer

- **October 29:**
  - Woke up with the idea for this book. Wrote frantically on my chalkboard wall because of all the ideas pouring out.
  - Set the goal to write and publish the book within 1 month.
- **November 21:**
  - Copy That Pops hit the 10,000 downloads marker and is not slowing down!
- **November 28:**
  - Launched this book on Amazon.
  - Hit #1 Amazon Best Seller. Woo!
- **December:**
  - Copy That Pops earned over 5,000 downloads in a single month.
- **2017:**
  - Started helping other entrepreneurs write, publish, and market best-selling books. Took 7 case studies plus video tutorials, checklists, and tools and turned it into an effective course!

    [Learn more at CopyThatPops.com].

1.8: Why Are There "Insights from Influencers" in This Book?

AS A TEACHER, YOU are never the be-all, end-all expert in whatever you are teaching, but rather a facilitator of the learning.

In my opinion, at least.

Just as I would include videos that others made, guest lectures, and supplemental readings in my lessons as an instructor, so too do I find this book to be more rich and useful to you, when my thoughts and experiences are enhanced by the insights of others.

Guest advice and examples come from other podcasting entrepreneurs and business owners with specializations in fields that directly help us with our goal to grow our podcasts, brands, and businesses.

We can all learn something from each of these people, and I thank them for their time and willingness to jump on board with my crazy write-a-book-in-one-month challenge. My first official book, no less.

Heartfelt gratitude to [in alphabetical order]:

- Adrian Aguilar (hear interview at CopyThatPops.com/050)

- Amanda Bond (hear interview at CopyThatPops.com/047)

- Andrew Steven

- Bernard Paraiso

- Brandon T. Adams (hear interview at CopyThatPops.com/046 and CopyThatPops.com/036)

- Elsie Escobar

- Jared Easley

- Jay Wong

- Jessica Kupferman

- Jessica Rhodes

- Jill Stanton (hear interview at CopyThatPops.com/049)

- John Lee Dumas (hear interview at CopyThatPops.com/052 and CopyThatPops.com/056)

- Khierstyn Ross

- Marcus Meurer (hear interview at CopyThatPops.com/044)

- Melissa Sue Tucker (hear interview at CopyThatPops.com/006)

- Michael O'Neal (hear interview at CopyThatPops.com/051)

- Stephen Christopher (hear interview at CopyThatPops.com/048)

- Stephen Dela Cruz (hear interview at CopyThatPops.com/043 and CopyThatPops.com/064)

- Yaro Starak

To kick things off, I want to highlight an influencer right here. Here are a few foundational words of wisdom for anyone planning to start a podcast or still struggling to get theirs to grow.

From my new friend and amazing podcaster, Jay Wong.

INSIGHTS FROM AN INFLUENCER: JAY WONG

Bio

Jay Wong is the Host and Executive Producer of The Inner Changemaker[12], an award-winning podcast where he interviews modern-day changemakers about choosing legacy over currency.

Prior guests include Bob Proctor, Sean Stephenson, Tucker Max, and many other world-class entrepreneurs.

Jay is dedicated to working with purpose-driven and passionate creators, helping them get their message out to the world in a BIGGER way.

He does this through his flagship podcast launch course "Podcast Your Brand," traveling the world podcasting, making videos documenting his journey, and running live seminars on personal branding and podcasting.

---

[12] http://www.theinnerchangemaker.com/

Some Brag-Worthy Stats

- His podcasting strategies have been featured in podcasting conferences throughout North America.

- Recognized by iTunes as the #1 podcast for self-improvement in 2015.

- Nominated as a Top 10 Business Podcast in 2016.

- In 2016, his podcast was even displayed on huge billboards at Yonge and Dundas Square in downtown Toronto for a week promoting the theme of "choosing legacy over currency."

~

Insight from Jay

"Start fast and launch with the intention that your show is going to make it BIG. Play to WIN and fail forward through this entire process.

Don't aim to be perfect. Be perfectly imperfect."

—

These pithy words of advice from Jay are just what we need to start us off!

Let's go fast, go big, and play to win!

So, let's grow!...I mean, go!

PART 2:
HOW TO GROW YOUR PODCAST, BRAND, AND BUSINESS WITH COMPELLING COPY

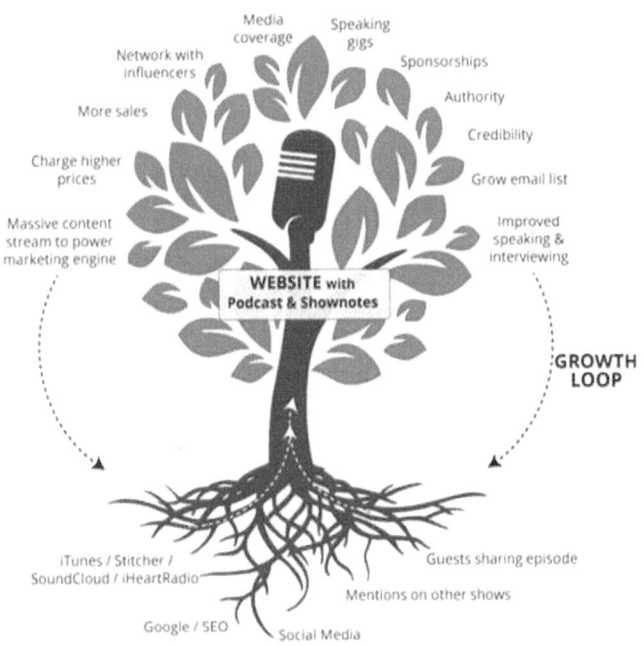

RESULTS

Media coverage

Speaking gigs

Network with influencers

Sponsorships

More sales

Authority

Charge higher prices

Credibility

Grow email list

Massive content stream to power marketing engine

Improved speaking & interviewing

WEBSITE with Podcast & Shownotes

GROWTH LOOP

iTunes / Stitcher / SoundCloud / iHeartRadio

Guests sharing episode

Mentions on other shows

Google / SEO

Social Media

TRAFFIC

2.1: It's Storytime

"Marketing is no longer about the stuff that you make but about the stories you tell."

~ Seth Godin

What is it?

ALLOW ME TO START off with a story. ;)

It was March of 2009 and I had just returned home after spending two weeks alone in Mexico.

Well, I went there alone, flying from Phoenix to Zihuatanejo, but I quickly made friends with another guy staying in the same hostel, who loved to play basketball each morning. We'd go shoot some hoops with the locals and a few expats and then pack up our stuff for a long, rough day of lying on a beautiful beach nearby.

It was just what I needed between semesters teaching teenagers about the Pythagorean Theorem and Cognitive Bias.

Two things made this trip more remarkable.

The 1st Thing

On the second to last night of my trip, I ran into a small group who I had met briefly, about 2 minutes passing by their dinner table, the night before. They told me how they were about to set sail (at 3:00 am that night), heading for Acapulco, about 153 miles south.

They invited me along and for some reason, I agreed. Getting on the boat in the middle of the night is not really like me, but it just felt right at the time. :)

After I grabbed my backpack and hopped on board, we slept a few hours, stretched out on the boat's seats under the night sky until others joined -- including the captain, a surprisingly young American man in his 30's, I forget his name now.

We set sail a bit later, maybe 4:00 am and I remember just lying there staring at the stars as we sailed away. I couldn't believe how gorgeous they were and how melodically the boat hummed along, bouncing gently from wave to wave.

I nodded off to sleep again until the captain woke us all up to watch the sunrise over the blue water.

Absolutely stunning.

As we continued to sail, hundreds of dolphins came over to swim and play and jump alongside the boat for a few miles. I have never seen anything like it since.

The trip took longer than expected, so we didn't get into Acapulco until far later than planned. I thought we'd have most of the day there, but instead we arrived about 10:00 pm and I had to catch a flight out of Zihuatanejo the next day!

Instead of heading right back to Zihuatanejo or at least get a hotel for the night, I decided, somewhat uncharacteristically, to dance, dance, dance with my new friends until about 3:00 am, jumping in a taxi just in time to catch the bus back to the airport up north and make my flight back home.

It was exhilarating. I felt free and alive.

The 2nd Thing

When I was back home and people asked about my two-week trip to Mexico, I recounted the story about the boat.

People were riveted by every detail and impressed by my gumption.

I realized right then that being able to tell a story had power.

Power to entertain.

Power to captivate.

Power to teach.

Power to stir emotion.

(Many members of my family were shocked and horrified at the, "Laura got on a boat with strangers in the middle of the night in Mexico" tagline.)

Even as I rewrite this story myself, I feel part of the exhilaration I felt in the moment and part of the fascination I remember eliciting from listeners of the story.

So, there is both an art and a science to telling a story that engages the listener or reader. And when done well, it can be an effective tool in your toolbelt for all areas of your business.

Why should podcasters care? Benefits to your brand and business

Storytelling is one of the things that make us unique in the animal kingdom, and it is a powerful force that psychologically binds us.

When we see or hear the beginnings of a good story, we tune out all other distractions to focus in and hear what comes next. We mentally insert ourselves into the story and live it vicariously in our minds.

Since we entrepreneurs "day trade attention" as Gary Vaynerchuk regularly says, we need attention to survive.

No traffic = no customers = no sales = no business.

So, as we go through the future chapters together looking at specific areas you need to write and write well to get attention and engagement for your podcast, brand, and business, remember just how powerful great storytelling can be.

It should permeate ALL of what you write, craft, and create with your podcast and beyond.

For me, it is far easier to entertain friends and family with stories from my travels than to craft "my story" in business.

Maybe because it feels safer to share about traveling than it does about my own journey as an entrepreneur.

Maybe some of you feel that way too?

If you read "My Story" in Part 1, you'll see that I built the foundation of my life at an early age around school and doing well academically.

So, it is NOT easy on my ego to talk about how long it took me to actually build a business that worked. It took far longer than I *thought* it should take based on my history of excelling in the academic system.

Turns out that school doesn't teach you some of the practical parts of life's success, am I right?

As an entrepreneur, I have guarded details of my true story for fear of looking dumb, foolish, and incapable. Of feeling like an imposter.

[Raise your hand if you've had an inkling of that ever?]

But the very act of hiding my true story surely contributed to my success taking longer than it could have because I was not owning it all and sharing it openly, which has so much power.

You attract more people with open authenticity than with generalities and half-truths.

I urge you to be more open to sharing your story and weaving elements of experiences into all that you do with your podcast (both verbally and in written form), in your webcopy, in your email nurture sequences, in social media, and more.

People make decisions based on emotion and justify them later with facts.

So use stories to extend a hand and bring people in.

INSIGHTS FROM AN INFLUENCER: BRANDON T. ADAMS

Bio

Brandon T. Adams[13] is Co-Host and Executive Producer of Ambitious Adventures[14], a reality television program focused on the compelling stories of young entrepreneurs.

In addition to his television work, Brandon is an entrepreneur through and through, owning a stake in a number of businesses including the Young Entrepreneur Convention, Keys to the Crowd, Arctic Stick, and an ice distributorship that serves 3 states.

As Founder and Host of the Live to Grind[15] podcast, a twice-weekly program that shines a light on successful entrepreneurs, Brandon delivers his unique brand of passionate

---

[13] http://brandontadams.com/
[14] http://ambitiousadventures.tv/
[15] http://livetogrind.com/podcast

motivation in his quest to impact 1 billion lives by the time he reaches 40 years old.

His work on the podcast inspired him to join with a group of other young professionals to form the Young Entrepreneur Convention. In its first year, the event drew nearly 500 attendees and featured speakers including Kevin Harrington of TV's "Shark Tank" and Priceline.com Founder Jeff Hoffman.

Brandon has also earned the moniker "King of Crowdfunding" for his work with clients launching products and services on crowdfunding platforms. Brandon and his Keys to the Crowd team have worked with high profile clients like Harrington, John Lee Dumas, as well as many others.

Brag-Worthy Stats:

- Worked with high-profile clients to raise over $1,000,000 in less than 12 months through crowdfunding

- One campaign raised almost $500,000 in 33 days for the 6th most-funded campaign of all time - John Lee Dumas's Freedom Journal

- Financial Advisor for the film THINK: The Legacy of Think and Grow Rich

- Crowdfunding campaign for THINK is the most funded docudrama in history

- Appeared on the cover of Inventors Digest

- Featured in Inc., USA Today, NBC, The Huffington Post

Advice from Brandon on Storytelling in General

When you tell a story, you need to be entertaining. People will remember stories. There are products out there that I buy just because I know the story behind it. Not because it's the best product. I didn't even care. I believed in the story and I remembered it.

Get people emotionally connected to the story. Show how you have been in situations where you have been in the shoes of your audience.

That's how you reach a lot of people. You have to tell your story throughout the podcast or web page copy. You have to show and tell your audience how your product or service will solve their problem and what they get for working with you.

Advice from Brandon on Getting Booked on Other Podcast Shows Using Your Stories

Tell your story from an angle that is unique compared to what else is being talked about on other shows. For me, I noticed that no one was talking about crowdfunding. So I showed how I was a crowdfunding expert through my story and how I was different.

That's how I got on Grant Cardone. I showed the results that I got with John Lee Dumas's Freedom Journal, and Grant wanted to do crowdfunding for real estate. No one else had presented that angle to him, so he brought me on.

Then it was an easier sell to Tai Lopez and others after that.

Once you get a lot of momentum, then you don't have to pitch as much and the opportunities come to you. but it starts with knowing and owning your story and how you are unique.

Brandon is right. Telling your story is incredibly important.

Take initiative from his example to get people to connect with you, see how you are different, and feel compelled to help share your message and mission.

INSIGHTS FROM AN INFLUENCER: STEPHEN DELA CRUZ

Bio

Stephen Dela Cruz is an entrepreneur, investor, speaker, podcaster, and coach.

He and his wife own 9 corporations and have 150 employees across the United States.

Right now, his main focuses are on their coaching business, writing their book, *The Lazy Millionaire*, and growing his podcast Success Talks - Stegela Success Mastery[16].

Insights from Stephen:

Stephen and I decided to do something unique to capture his insights.

We did a quick interview on the topic and I'm including the transcript of our conversation with the advice regarding storytelling and its importance below.

To listen to the full episode, head over to http://CopyThatPops/043

---

[16] http://www.stegelasuccess.com/podcast/

Stephen:

So, I love sales and there's a quote that I absolutely love, a sales guru said, "Facts tell, stories sell."

And it's the aspect that what people buy is rarely off of logic. A lot of times people buy off emotion.

And emotion is stirred by a story and if any kind of story out there can be relatable, our human mind looks for ways to be relating to that story. Even if it's not their personal experience, they say, "Oh, my friend Barbara went through the exact same thing."

Even though it's not their story, they're still thinking, "Oh, wow this relates to my friend which in somehow relates to me."

So when someone tells a story, we're listening or grasping onto it because we're trying to find some emotion to feel about it, and if Barbara stirs emotion and you feel sorry for Barbara, then you also feel sorry for that story. We really try to find a way to relate.

So, I really love the idea that facts tell, stories sell.

I'm hiring now, for example. I'm hiring a sales team for one of my companies and I tell them to tell me a story about their life 'on this particular product.'

They get kind of weirded out, they say 'what?'

I say, "I don't want you to convince me with the logic, I want you to convince me with your story. How does it relate to you?"

If it doesn't relate to you then you shouldn't be selling this product because there's no personal touch to it. I believe that stories add that personal touch.

So, if you're going to a jeweler and the jeweler says, "Oh my gosh, yes, my wife loves the exact same diamond bracelet. We saw it in Paris and ..."

Now there's some kind of story attached to whatever it is you're trying to sell. Then that person buying it will go, "Awe, okay. I see. I'll take it too."

They're no longer just buying that product, but they're also buying that story.

So, when it comes to podcasts, because that's the whole topic here, I love it when I listen to a podcast when someone goes through a story and I think, "Wow, that's a whole podcast, that went by so quickly!"

Laura:

Yeah.

Stephen:

Because you're following them in their whole journey and that's what I love about it. That's what I love about these podcasts that have interviews.

The interviews are all different so a lot of times it's the interviewee sharing their story, so then we just grasp onto it.

We love it because we are in a reality TV generation where everyone doesn't like scripted; they want the real story, they want the real deal.

The real emotions, what happened in someone else's life because we're all looking for that comfort, wondering "Am I alone?"

"Does this person relate to me?"

And so we're trying to grasp onto that. So I believe that the more we tell stories, the more we become relatable.

Laura:

That's perfect. I'm even thinking of questions to go deeper if you're good with that?

What's a story that you tell often that you find your audience people really resonate with?

Stephen:

Right, so when it comes to me, I have multiple stories. I would say right now though, my story now, this very present moment is I'm really pushing, because I have 9 corporations. I have daycares, I have real estate, I have talent agencies and all this other stuff going on.

But right now my main focus on is Stegela Success Mastery, which is my coaching program and my mastermind group here in San Diego.

And my story behind that is in 2015, last year, February, it was Valentine's actually, I had a stroke.

When I had my stroke, the paramedic guy -- back then I used to live in La Jolla -- said "Wow, this is a really nice area. You live in a nice place."

And I thought they were trying to probably just small talk to keep me engaged but at the back of my head I'm like, "My whole body is freaking numb, like take me to the hospital! I don't want to discuss about where I live."

Laura:

Yeah.

Stephen:

And then on the drive to the hospital, they said, "Man, you're a very lucky guy. You're only 28 years old and you live here in La Jolla. Nice view... yeah, yeah, yeah."

And that got me thinking in the back of mind, like wow, if today was my last day today, because I don't know what's going on, all I have to leave back behind is money and that's not really a gold star to put by your name.

So, sure money is great but money comes and goes, so once that money has been spent, there you go.

That's where I really decided right there and then, life isn't about making money, because I almost lost my whole life.

I really said to myself, "Okay, you know what? I've got to refocus my entire life and I'm still going to hustle and everything but now my whole focus is not just success but success with significance."

So we went to Thrive a couple weeks ago and that really resonated so much with me and I'm so glad I went.

Now my whole theme in my life now is no longer hustling for the money, but now more for how am I going to leave a legacy?

How am I going to touch people's lives?

And I have such a passion for entrepreneurship, been doing it for so long, at a young age. So I have a passion for those to leave their 9 to 5, quit building someone else's dream, and start building your own.

So that's where I'm at right now, my passion and that's the story I tell is my whole scare last year.

Through my health. So, I don't know if anyone can relate to that but a lot of times people tell me, "Oh, I relate to that because my dad had a stroke" or like, "Wow, I've got to figure out my own health because I'm young too."

Laura:

Right.

Stephen:

It really gives a lot of contemplation, a lot of reflection but there's now more meaning behind what I do.

So, I'm telling someone to sign up for my program or whatever else, there's a little more emotion rather than just an 'ah, no this is too expensive.'

So, they're not buying by price.

Laura:

Right.

Stephen:

A little side note with this: 3 reasons why people buy or don't buy is 3 P's.

The person, the product, or the price.

With that being said, the big major factor is not the product or the price; the main factor is the person.

If the person can charm you, that person can really reel you in, you build rapport with them, then the product and the price is easy-peasy.

If you look at the mall, for example. These guys who are trying to hand you lotion, they're really trying to make that connection.

Eye contact. "How are you?"

"Very nice blouse on today."

Whatever else they can make a connection with you somehow, someway. So that's the whole thing. But a lot of times what really works in that kind of atmosphere of the mall is not 'you have a nice blouse' or 'hey, take a look at my product, take the sample,' but it's really more like a 'Hey, how are you?'

Then that creates conversation.

That's the whole aspect with sales and stories and my story. The way I use it.

Laura:

That's great feedback. Did you try other stories and realize that that one was really resonating more than others or ...?

Stephen:

You know, honestly, I didn't. We had a whole mastermind behind this about 'what is your story?' What product are you pushing and what story do you have?

We really had to sit down and purposefully think about different stories that we had that could resonate with this.

So yes, this is a real story, my own story, and yes those thoughts did come up to me but there really is actually is my 'why,' why I started Stegela

Success Mastery, and so I can be focused on other real estate properties, other business ventures but this is something I really want to push into, which is the educational realm, because primarily of this reason.

But for those who don't have that... well why am I selling sneakers or why am I pushing for this product or this book or this whatever?

It really comes down to deeper, there's an awesome course out there. I think you can download it on YouTube actually, just Google it, Seven Levels of Why.

It digs really, really, really, really deep to what is your why.

When someone says, "What is your why?" "I want to leave a legacy for my family."

Well, it goes sooooo deep, like seven levels of why.

And out of that why, when you go that deep into it, you'll find the real core behind it.

It comes down to always your past, your childhood, or a lot of times it comes to the fear of regret. And Tony Robbins says there's two things that are a driving force for us: pleasure or pain. Out of that comes passion. Because of one of those two things.

So that is what I'd say is a good way to create your story, is to figure out a deep, deep level.

What is your why?

Why are you selling your sneakers?

Why are you selling X, Y, Z?

Why are you pushing this product?

Why are you doing what you're doing?

Not just 'I'm doing it to make money,' but it's beyond that. You can make money anywhere, but why particularly that?

Laura:

I love that suggestion and that's actually something that I feel like I could improve on.

So I'm now thinking I'll Google this and actually do it and maybe even include it in the book and just say, "Hey, my story is I didn't have a story 100%, let's figure it out together and here you can see it happening and unfolding" and maybe people could walk through it.

[Go to book freebies[17] to see what I wrote out as I watched the video].

Stephen:

And the more vulnerable we are, the better that people connect with us.

So it really comes down to, "You know what? My marriage is on the rocks for this particular situation and if I had this product then it would have totally transformed everything. So now I want to provide this because I couldn't find it back in the day."

Everyone goes through stuff, everyone goes through so much pain, so it's just a matter of finding that thing how can it be relatable to people?

---

[17] http://www.podcastteachers.com/book-freebies/

Laura:

Awesome, I love it. Very good advice for the book and for in general!

Stephen:

Very cool.

So true, Stephen! I am so glad that your health is back on track and you are growing your business with passion and purpose.

Okay [reader], let's talk about how to find and use YOUR story in the next section.

How to implement this right now

Step 1: Open up a Google Spreadsheet[18] (or use Excel, if you must! :)

-- I don't like attachments anymore and have switched to all digital).

Step 2: In a column, list out in short words and phrases all the momentous moments in your life.

[See "My Story" in Chapter 1.7 for an example].

Step 3: In a column to the right of the first one, note what you learned from each of these moments, especially as it relates to your current podcast and business.

Step 4: Pick out your top 5 of the above.

Look for ones that are pivotal moments in your life and where emotion stirs in you as you think about it and write about it. Look for elements that make you different from others in your space.

Step 5: Rewrite these 5 on a fresh tab and bookmark the document or rewrite the 5 on a sticky note and stick it on your computer or a wall where you can easily see it every day.

---

[18] https://www.google.com/sheets/about/

Step 6: Little by little, start working these 5 stories into conversations, web copy, email sequences, podcast episodes, and Facebook comments (where appropriate).

Step 7: Own these stories and practice telling them. Watch how people react and respond. Revise how you tell them to convey the message even more powerfully.

Remember these stories as we work through the chapters that come.

Pop Quiz

1. T/F: Not everyone has stories.

2. T/F: You're either good at telling stories or you aren't.

3. T/F: 'Different' is often better than 'better'.

Answers:

1. F – We all have stories!

2. F – Practice!

3. T – Find how you are different and work it into your stories.

2.2: Show-Stopping Shownames

A SHOWNAME IS ONE of the key pieces of your podcast. People ask you all the time, "Oh, what's your show called?"

So you need to put thought and effort into choosing the right one.

Easier said than done! :)

Let's look at it together.

Why should podcasters care? Benefits to your brand and business

Your showname is to your podcast like a headline is to a blog post.

Or a title is to a movie or a book.

It's the first thing people are going to see (along with the artwork), or hear, when exposed to your show.

According to research out of Princeton, all it takes is 1/10th of a second to form an impression of a stranger from their face. And being exposed to the face longer does not significantly change those impressions, but they can reinforce your confidence in your gut reaction[19].

This is for faces, not for podcast shownames, but we can extrapolate that forming fast gut reactions about new things is not unique to faces.

Plus, raise your hand if you have ever gone looking for something online or in your phone and two minutes later you are somewhere else completely and have no idea what you were there for in the first place.

My hand is raised.

Even online, even with our podcasts and businesses, we have a short time to make a good first impression and be memorable. The name of your show is a big component of that.

---

[19] https://www.princeton.edu/main/news/archive/ S15/62/69K40/index.xml?section=topstories

Picking a name that is hard to pronounce, easy to misspell, unrelated to your topic, or crazy long (without purpose) loses people immediately.

And then confirmation bias kicks in. This is our tendency to look for information that reinforces our beliefs. Get off to a bad start and others will be looking for other reasons to support their disinterest or confusion and bounce.

Your showname is also being indexed by search engine bots like Google and iTunes. So being mindful of keywords that you are wanting to rank for is important.

Pro Tip:

If you aren't super creative and don't have the budget to pay for a branding and creative team, stick with more literal names that include keywords your audience would actually search for.

Quick self-reflection from an influencer we hear from later in the book

"60 Seconds of Solitude is cute and all, but I would have had more luck calling my show 1 Minute Meditation because people are searching for 'meditation.' They aren't searching for 'solitude.' lol"

~ Melissa Sue Tucker

Laura's experience

Picking a showname is actually something that took me the longest when I was trying to name my show "Copy That Pops." Even to this day I am always thinking of new ideas for different name options. But eventually, as you know, you just have to pick something and move forward.

Progress is better than perfection.

When I was trying to decide on the name for my show, I was conscientious of four things:

1. Keywords
2. Brevity
3. What URL was still available
4. Catchiness

1. Keywords

In my show I talk about copywriting tips and applying Psychology. And the ways to communicate about your business and brand better online. So, I felt compelled to communicate that in the title of my show. Hence the use of the word "copy."

The reason this is a good idea is two-fold.

1) If someone comes to your show without knowing anything about you or your business, the showname and the show art are the first things that they're going to see.

So it is helpful to have some words in the title that clue them into what you're all about and let them know right away that they're in the right place to get the type of information they're looking for.

2) If somebody is searching for a keyword that you do cover and it's also in your same name it's going to increase the likelihood that you come up in the search.

Of course optimizing for search is far more complex than just the words in your title but it certainly can help.

2. Brevity

In terms of being concise, I ended up deciding to avoid words like "entrepreneur" because that word is so long and actually difficult to spell for most people. Even I mess it up and I'm writing it nearly every single day. Is it "entrepreneur" or "entreprenuer"!?!?

One successful business friend of mine even said that he tries his hardest to come up with a name that is only two syllables.

While that is not always feasible, it's good to keep in mind that shorter is usually better.

So be thoughtful about the words that you choose and see where you can cut out unnecessary words or select synonyms that are shorter if they still capture the essence of what your show will be all about.

3. URL Availability

Third, I wanted to pick a showname for which I could still get the URL with the .com. This proved to be the most troublesome factor of the four and I ended up throwing away a lot of good ideas just because I couldn't get the URL.

But some people work around that by adding the word podcast after their show's name or at least just after the show inside of the URL in order to get the .com.

For example, if your name is Jen and your show is called "Eating Healthy" but www.EatingHealthy.com is already taken, you could grab up the URL "EatingHealthyPodcast.com" or "EatingHealthywithJen.com."

If you already have a website, another option is to simply create another page on the website you already have and brand with your podcast name, not even worrying about a new URL.

For example, when Melissa Sue Tucker and I launch our Podcast Teachers' podcast, we will just put it at PodcastTeachers.com/podcast no matter what name variation we may use. Though I plan to be more literal with that one.

4. Catchiness

Lastly, you want to keep in mind a name that is going to entice a new visitor to turn into a listener.

So put on your creative thinking caps and try to be playful with some of the ideas you already have and see if you can tweak your ideas to be a bit more unique, a bit more captivating.

Part of the reason I like the name "Copy That Pops" is because the word "copy" and the word "pop" make the same vowel sound, which I find melodic.

I also heard the advice many years ago about choosing words that are heavier on consonants than on vowels, where possible. While certainly not a hard-and-fast rule, see if keeping that in mind inspires you to any other combination that sounds more powerful and punchy.

Great examples

1. The first example I'd like to highlight is She Podcasts.

Note: Jump to Insights from an Influencer to hear the story behind this name!

From just the title, you get:

- "She" = female, women, lady power
- "Podcasts" = podcasting

Plus, it is short and punchy. There are no unnecessary words, no ambiguity.

Elsie Escobar and Jessica Kupferman -- the hosts and creators -- clearly know their target audience and have nailed it with a showname that has keywords, is brief, they got the URL, and is catchy too.

It hits all four of the criteria for a great showname.

And once you listen, you see they also deliver on the promise of their showname so they are aligned.

Great job, She Podcasts!

2. The second is my personal favorite podcast, The Tim Ferriss Show

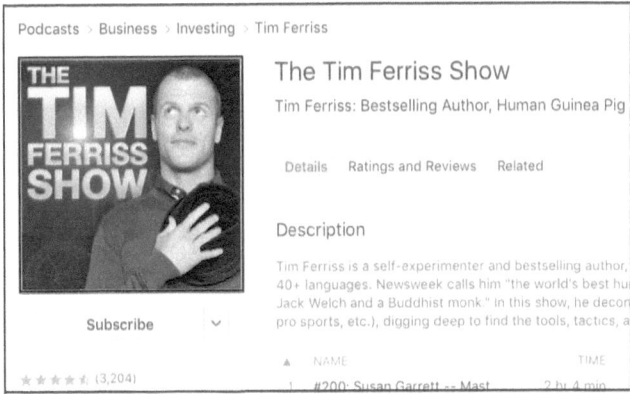

From the title, you obviously get that Tim is the central glue of this show.

He even described in a podcast episode why he named the show with his name instead of something else [arguably] more creative.

He knew that his show was going to be a mix of a lot of things and wanted to be free to experiment and not feel trapped because of a naming decision early on.

At the time of this writing, he has 200 episodes published and he has had this kind of variety:

Interviews with:

- Actors like Arnold Schwarzenegger and Jamie Foxx
- Authors like Scott Adams, the creator of the comic Dilbert
- Athletes like Amelia Boone and Gabrielle Reese
- Big names in business like Seth Godin and Tony Robbins

Plus non-interviews episodes like:

- Drunk dialing fans and answering their questions
- Recording a how-to session around acroyoga
- Readings from Senaca, the stoic philosopher
- Best 5 tools for sleep

Tim realized that the decision around a showname could be potentially limiting if too narrow.

Plus, he has the luxury of a huge audience already, so including his name helps with name recognition.

If you do not have a huge audience yet, using your own name will not have quite the effect that Tim got, but it is still worth considering, depending on your branding and business goals.

3. The third is WTF with Marc Maron

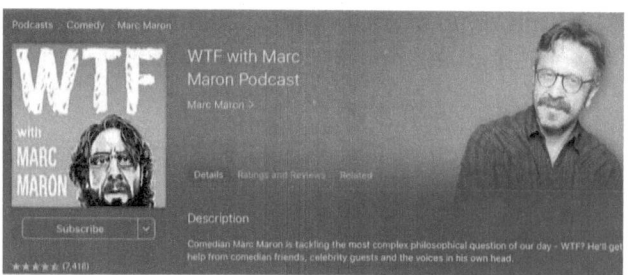

I find the title of "WTF" funny and appropriate.

If you are not sure what WTF stands for, allow me to break it down.

W = What

T = The

F = [expletive]

So, from this name alone, you get the message that there will be cursing, it is probably funny, and the topics are likely broad.

What are some of your favorite shows with great shownames? Snap me @LaptopLaura on Snapchat to let me know!

INSIGHTS FROM INFLUENCERS:
ELSIE AND JESS - SHE PODCATS

Background

She Podcasts[20] began in 2014 as a small Facebook group[21], built so that their women podcaster friends could have a place online to get quick podcasting answers, tips, and resources from one another.

However, as soon as the group started, it grew enormously. Friends added friends and it now has about 4,500 women in some phase of building and producing a podcast at the time of this writing.

In the spirit of further support, a podcast was created to address issues and podcasting current events as they relate to women.

---

[20] https://www.shepodcasts.com/
[21] https://www.facebook.com/groups/shepodcasts/

Hosted by Elsie Escobar and Jessica Kupferman, She Podcasts is doing fabulously well and representing powerful female voices in podcasting.

Elsie Escobar Bio

With a background in theatre, film, and T.V., Elsie Escobar works in the cross-section of technology, digital media, and holistic living with a heavy bias on podcast production and the creative use of audio. Her services include Digital Media Strategy and Development with a strong podcasting focus and creating powerful innovative digital media strategies that build community.

Elsie is Co-founder of the Podcasting School For Women[22], Co-founder and Co-host of She Podcasts, and Co-host of The Feed: The Official Libsyn Podcast[23], whose key focus is on keeping podcasters podcasting.

She is also the Social Media Community Manager at Libsyn, the world's largest podcast network and host, and an inaugural member of the Academy of Podcasters.

Jessica Kupferman Bio

Jessica Kupferman is a Digital Media Strategist with over 15 years of experience working in the internet marketing space. Combining a mix of creativity and business development, Jessica works with large companies (like Comcast, Subaru, Leisure Fitness, and Bank of America), small businesses, and podcasters who want fresh ways of selling and growing online.

---

[22] http://shepodcasts.teachable.com/p/psfw
[23] https://itunes.apple.com/au/podcast/feed-official-libsyn-podcast/id668413144?mt=2

Jessica is Co-founder of the Podcasting School For Women and Co-founder and Co-host of She Podcasts.

She has been has been featured on The Social Media Examiner, Entrepreneur.com, TMZ, Entrepreneur On Fire, and many more.

She is an experienced, sought-after speaker and podcaster, known for her humor and tell-it-like-it-is personality. She is also an inaugural member of the Academy of Podcasters.

The Story Behind the Name "She Podcasts"

From Elsie Escobar:

"I came up with the name.

I'd been dreaming about doing a podcast that showcased women podcasters in some way for years. My original idea was to do something like Rob Walch's podCast411[24] but focusing on women podcasters.

I used to daydream about the show and the name came to me all at once. I filed it away for a possible future project.

I knew how hard it was to *keep podcasting* and didn't want to make a commitment to a podcast until the time was right.

Then, Jessica, my partner in crime came into the mix. We chatted about making a podcast that was aimed at women podcasters and I thought 'She Podcasts' would be perfect.

And so it was!"

---

[24] http://podcast411.libsyn.com/

As with Elsie, inspiration for the perfect name can strike suddenly, so have a tool handy to capture great ideas for when you are ready for them!

INSIGHTS FROM AN INFLUENCER: JOHN LEE DUMAS

If you are even remotely interested in podcasting and are an entrepreneur, you have heard of this section's major influencer. He is the reigning King of Podcasting in this space, and I am honored to include his stories and advice in this book.

Bio

John Lee Dumas is the Founder and Host of EOFire[25] (Entrepreneur On Fire), an award-winning podcast where he interviews today's most inspiring

entrepreneurs 7-days a week!

EOFire was awarded Best of iTunes and with over 1500 episodes at the time of this writing, he's shared a ton of great content!

EOFire has featured incredible entrepreneurs such as Tony Robbins, Seth Godin, Gary Vaynerchuk, Barbara Corcoran, Tim Ferriss, Brian Tracy, Guy Kawasaki, Pat Flynn, and so many more.

Other Brag-Worthy Stats

- Author of *Podcast Launch* (#1 results on Amazon for podcasting)
- Runs Podcasters' Paradise, an incredible membership site for podcasters who want to

---

[25] http://www.eofire.com/

learn all the ins and outs of podcasting from start to growth

- Awarded "Best of iTunes 2013"
- Hit 1 millions listens in A SINGLE MONTH in January of 2015
- Keynote speaker at Podcast Movement, Young Entrepreneur's Convention, Social Media Marketing World, and more.
- Launched the 6th most funded Kickstarter campaign ever for The Freedom Journal in 2016
- Earned over $154,000 net *income* last month (October 2016)

Insights from John Lee Dumas (JLD)

I asked this influencer to jump on a quick Skype call to record his answers to a few questions.

Check out http://copythatpops.com/052 to hear the full audio interview.

Below is an excerpt from that conversation about show-stopping shownames.

Learn from JLD's story!

Laura:

Tell me about the story of how you came up with Entrepreneur On Fire.

John:

I'm a big believer when it comes to shownames that you want to be both clear and clever if possible, but always, always lean towards clear if you have to choose between the two.

For me, I just knew that I wanted my podcast to serve entrepreneurs, to interview entrepreneurs, and so I knew that I wanted to rank for the keyword 'entrepreneur.'

That was really what led into me looking how could I build a showname around the word entrepreneur. I really wanted that to be the first and foremost name, so I knew I wanted that to be in the first position, but then I was trying to think of what could come after that.

To be honest with you, I was watching SportsCenter one night, and the late, great Stuart Scott goes, "LeBron James is on fire!" and it just kind of hit me. That is a phrase, the words "on fire," that people just get internationally.

They know that it means like you're in the zone, you're crushing it, so that was where the name Entrepreneur On Fire came.

Of course, we since moved into EOFire as the brand's evolved and just kind of became a stand alone. It's much easier to go to EOFire.com than to try to spell the word entrepreneur, which was always a struggle, so something you should think of as well when you're coming up with a showname.

Is it something that is easily spellable? And the word entrepreneur wasn't, but it was too important of a word for me not to use at the beginning.

Laura:

That makes so much sense. I actually thought about that for my own show, too, using entrepreneur, but kind of went away from it for those reasons you described.

And actually, my second question was around your switch to EOFire. Did you notice anything particularly good or maybe even bad in terms of increased traffic, brand recognition, or business growth when you made that switch?

John:

There was good and bad. You know, the good first and foremost was that it was just easier to get to that domain, EOFire.com slash whatever. It just kind of rolls off the tongue and it just made a lot more sense.

For me, I wanted my name to come out from behind the shadows where it started, because it started with just Entrepreneur On Fire. And "Inspiring Millions" was the tagline.

We switched it to basically Entrepreneur On Fire with John Lee Dumas, but then we wanted to continue to bring my name and my individual brand to the forefront.

Taking the emphasis off of the word 'entrepreneur' and putting it on EOFire John Lee Dumas. Now that is the logo, that's the brand, and that's really where we want it to stay for the foreseeable future.

There definitely was some negatives as well. A lot of people still refer to the show as Entrepreneur On Fire and always will, which is totally fine, like we own that domain, EntrepreneurOnFire.com, which just forwards to EOFire.com.

They also would tell their friends about it and their friends might go searching for it, and be like, "Oh, my friend told me about Entrepreneur On Fire. I'm not finding it." Because they're not going to associate EOFire with Entrepreneur On Fire. There definitely was some negatives and some cons to doing the switch as well, but it's been a couple years now and we're pretty happy with the switch over all.

Laura's Takeaways from John Lee Dumas's insights:

John brought up some great points about a top showname.

1. Be clear, first and foremost.

2. Then try to be clever and memorable too, if you can. But not at the cost of clarity.

3. Keep keywords that you want to rank highly for in mind.

4. Consider branding now and long-term.

5. But know that you can always adjust as you grow and learn.

Amazing!

INSIGHTS FROM AN INFLUENCER: MICHAEL O'NEAL

Bio

Michael is a mid-western kid turned San Diego native and host of Proudly Unemployable - The Solopreneur Hour podcast[26] where he interviews the best and the brightest solopreneurs from all walks of life, including internet marketing, network marketing, music, fitness, T.V. and film, comedy, and more.

Michael is also a coveted speaker and emcee with over 18 years of experience in branding, web design, and social media marketing consulting.

Brag-Worthy Stats

- Hit iTunes Top 10 Business List within the first month of airing

- Nominated as a "Best New Show in 2013" by Stitcher Radio

- Named in the "35 Outstanding Podcast Picks for Entrepreneurs Like You" by Inc. Magazine

---

[26] https://solopreneurhour.com/

- Named in the "100 Podcasts That Will Make You Smarter, Better, and Wiser" by Inc. Magazine
- Recorded over 500 episodes and earned 8 million downloads

Direct Advice from Michael

The transcript below is an excerpt from a conversation that Michael and I had in late November, 2016. It is also at http://copythatpops.com/051 if you want to hear it in full.

Worth a listen!

Michael brings years of experience using words to convey complex meanings and drive revenue. There is so much to be learned from this proudly unemployable podcasting solopreneur.

—

Laura:

What's the story behind your coming up with The Solopreneur Hour?

Michael:

Well, I had been in that world for a long time. When I started in the podcast world, it was because I knew a dude that was an amazing speaker, like public speaker. He was a big mindset coach.

I would watch him speak in front of 10,000 people and you could hear a pin drop. It's one thing to get a crowd all hyped up, it's another to make them silent. That's when you know someone has a real command of a room.

He came to me with a YouTube question years ago. This was 2011. He said he had this very specific YouTube question. I said, "David, I can answer that, but I've seen you now speak in front of thousands of people, and you really command the room. We should really think about growing your brand."

And he goes, "How do we do that?" I said, "What about a podcast?" He said, "What's a podcast?" I said, "It's like a radio show. You download it."

So, I created this show called The Kickass Life with David Wood. It became a hit. It was in the self-help section of iTunes and it was always Top 10.

And I'd met so many people through not only the workings of that show, but just prior, people that were super successful with their own niche businesses, anyone from affiliate marketers to network marketers to real estate agents to actors and to comedians to whatever.

These were people that would be C-level people, CEO, COO, those kinds of types at a regular company, but they weren't interested in the corporate world. But I always found them very fascinating and very generous with their time, and I just knew I wanted to be around those kinds of people.

I didn't know what the common thread was, though. And when I had the idea of doing a show, I knew I wanted to talk to these people, but I didn't know why. I didn't know what the story was behind all of them.

I was on my bike. I was here in San Diego. I was riding in Ocean Beach, and I heard someone advertise ...I want to say it was like the MacNeil/Lehrer Hour or something like that.

And I said, "Oh, my God, The Solopreneur Hour. That's what they are. I'm going to talk to these people for an hour and the fact that they're all solopreneurs is the common thread, because ultimately, when you hire their business, you're really getting them."

And that's how I define solopreneur.

Like I said, that could encapsulate an actor or a comedian or an athlete or a musician or a real estate agent, or whatever. They all have to follow very similar branding and marketing protocols to be successful in their businesses no matter what they are.

So, I said, "What if I just focus on the similarities between all of those different career engines?" and that's the show.

That's really the origin of why I named it that. Plus, I was a designer and a branding guy for 18 years before I started all these shenanigans.

Laura:

Oh, nice.

Michael:

Yeah. I knew a lot about the power of words. In fact, when I talk to people about brand, I just went through a branding exercise with my girlfriend this weekend, and I said ... It's so interesting how people interpret these things. I'll do it to you now.

Laura:

Sure.

Michael:

If you close your eyes, what do you think of when I say the word "bank"?

Laura:

I see a money sign and a building that's brick or grayish brick.

Michael:

What else? Just keep describing what you see.

Laura:

I see people in suits, mostly men, unfortunately. [laughs]

Michael:

Okay. What about a library?

Laura:

I see a librarian, female with glasses sitting behind a desk, books everywhere, dim lighting, not very bright. Warm, lots of brown, muted colors.

Michael:

Umm. All right. A couple things that are really cool about words. Both of those words have a lot of power in them. On a psychological standpoint, I can tell right away you're a visual learner, you like things visual.

That's how you describe things. We could deep dive into some of the other narratives, but you are very visual on how you process. My girlfriend is very kinesthetic in how she processes.

Laura:

So, how did she answer it?

Michael:

She described it with paying bills. She did all the -

Laura:

Oh, like actions.

Michael:

Actions. Reading books. She didn't, for a second, see a library or a bank. I'm like you. I see a library and a bank and I describe the marble and here's the vault, and that's what I see.

But she interpreted the action items associated with those things. What's cool about all of that is that was 1 word!

Laura:

Yeah!

Michael:

When we think of a brand and how powerful a word is, when I think of The Solopreneur Hour, it tells the story, especially if they see the tagline, which is Job Security for the Unemployable, or the more updated version, which is Proudly Unemployable.

So, when someone sees those two words juxtaposed, and it really is a juxtaposition because people initially think, "Oh, you're unemployable. You're difficult to work. You don't want to work," but when they see "proudly" in front of that word, they go, "Oh, wait a second. There's more to it than that."

If I'm proudly unemployable, it means I'm probably an entrepreneur. I probably have no desire to be employed.

That, to me, is really the fun of digging into words and how powerful they can be for representing not only someone's brand, but someone's show and that kind of thing.

Laura:

I love that. That was my follow up question to that thread, was about the "proudly unemployable," because the first time I heard that, I was just like, "That's amazing. It just captures it," because I feel that way, too. I would never go back to another job unless I literally was about to starve to death, and I don't see that happening. So, I totally resonate with those words together.

Michael:

Right. When you see it, when you first go through that process of bank and library, and then you see something like "proudly unemployable," you go, "Oh, wow! That actually tells the whole story. I can visualize what that means now that I know the background of it." And that's what's cool.

Laura:

Can you think of any advice for someone who's sitting down to maybe write a show name right now and they've maybe written out tons of word, and they're just like, "I can't come up with something that's so clear and clever at the same time"?

Do you have any advice for other activities they could do or ways they could brainstorm and put something together?

Michael:

Yeah. First and foremost, just know that this is something I did for a living. The branding exercise that I did with my girlfriend, without kidding, we would have charged $25,000 for my agency. The thing we had at the table going through the process of would have been a huge process at an agency.

I've obviously made a Twitter version of it for her and we just banged it out, but despite my background in all of this stuff, it took me three months to come up with The Solopreneur Hour, like solid three months of pouring...so, if you don't get it in a night or a weekend, don't be frustrated, first and foremost, because harnessing the power of words is very difficult sometimes.

As we went through the process, there's a lot of thesaurus.com, there's a lot of ... In fact, I could tell you how we landed. She's an RN. She's a very, very high-end RN, meaning she's not only trained in the RN stuff, but has a lot of other ... your know, she goes to seminars all the time, so she's very well-skilled in the ICU and PICU, which is the little kids' ICU and all those things, but then also has this huge eastern medicine philosophy. She knows all about holistic nutrition. So, she's starting a business to combine all of those things.

I said, "Before we find out ... " and this goes for anybody's brand, before you start you've got to figure out what are the pain points of your audience. Right?

When someone sees my shirt that says, "I am unemployable," I get people walk up to me all the time and go, "Oh, my God. I'm totally unemployable." That's a pain point for them.

So, what we - I just did a couple of Facebook posts -

Laura:

I saw those.

Michael:

What we saw ... And people didn't know why I was doing it. I just wanted -- I had this one friend of mine who kept defending. I'm like, "Stop defending. This is not about that. I'm just trying to get some feedback here."

It was really funny actually, but people didn't feel heard, people didn't feel like modern medicine knew enough about nutrition, and they didn't feel like there was enough one-to-one interactions.

We came up, we said, "All right. Here's what we know that she's going to do." She knows a ton about holistic nutrition, she knows a ton about actual supplements, and she can do it with blood tests. So, she can see what's wrong and supplement the things that are necessary, which is the real edge that an RN has versus someone who's just more nutrition-based. She can actually see the blood tests behind it.

And then she does a process called healing touch, which is a therapeutic technique actually taught in the hospital, but it's very eastern, it's very energy-based. Then she actually listens. She's someone who will sit and listen to people and how they feel in their body. She'll listen to that.

So I said, "All right. Those are those four elements." We took about two hours going through all the websites and words and things like that.

We ended up with Remedy Recipe.

The name of her company's now called Remedy Recipe. The logo is this really cool, old school medical bag that has icons for each of those four different things: touch, listening, nutrition, and supplementation. Each has its own individual icon. It looks great. It's green and pink and it represents her really well. That's something that would be the process of it.

I really love a book called *Zag* by Marty Neumeier. "When everyone else zigs, you zag." It's about finding white space in the market and really defining your brand. I have a group of books called the Sexy Seven. It's the seventh book.

Laura:

That's a clever name, too!

Awesome advice, Michael! Thanks! The $25,000 check for this branding session is in the mail.

How to implement this right now

Activity

Now that you have some solid tips and examples in mind, let's get brainstorming.

Even if you already have a showname, this is still a good exercise. You may come up with something even better and be compelled to do a rebrand. There's nothing saying you can't. It's your show.

Step 1: Clear your world of distractions.

- put your phone on airplane mode
- silence notifications from your computer
- shut the door and hang a 'do not disturb sign'

Step 2: Put 20 minutes on a timer.

Step 3: Put pen to paper or type into a Google Doc, and write out all the words that feel right to describe you the host, the topics you're going to discuss on the show, the types of people who are going to listen to your show, and anything else that pops into your mind. You can also write in the lines provided below:

_____

_____

_____

_____

_____

Important Note:

During your first brainstorm session you don't want to edit yourself; you don't want to restrict yourself. Just write anything that comes to mind. Let it be a free-write session.

Step 4: After doing this for about 20 minutes, open up thesaurus.com in a browser window and type in some of the top of words that you keep thinking about over and over. Plug them in and see what other synonyms you haven't considered yet.

Step 5: Put 5 minutes on the timer.

Step 6: Write down the synonyms you hadn't yet considered and play with new combinations.

_____

_____

_____

_____

_____

_____

_____

_____

_____

From this exercise, you're going to produce a lot of creative ideas.

Step 7: Moving forward I would suggest selecting your top 4 or 5 and then taking it back to your tribe, your community online, your friends and family even. Ask for their feedback.

Consider asking things like:

> ➢ Which grabs your attention the most?

> ➢ What do you think about when you hear this name?

Remember though that the opinions that matter the most are from those who are in your target audience. So be careful to not give too much weight to the opinion of those who are not in your target market. I think it would be terrible to throw out a killer idea that your audience would rave about and resonate with just because someone close to you in your life "didn't get it."

And let me share a personal story on this, that is slightly funny and maybe embarrassing, but what the heck.

After I had selected the name "Copy That Pops" and got feedback from my audience, a couple of people made the comment that they read the name as "Copy That, Pops" as in "I have heard and understood, Dad"! [Instead of my intention of "Copy, That Pops" or "Writing and Communication that is Catchy and Intriguing."

That thought had NEVER occurred to me before and I had a laugh. But since the people who read it that way were outside my target audience (mostly male and in their 40's to 60's), I decided to plow ahead anyhow. Most of my audience is female in their 20's and 30's, so most of them do not readily think of hand-radios and calling their dads "pops." :)

So, this is a funny example of getting feedback and really trying to see how others perceive your showname.

It does matter.

Pop Quiz

1. What is your showname?

   _____

2. Does it hit the mark for keywords, brevity, URL address, and catchiness?

   _____

   _____

3. What feedback did you get from your target market?

   [If not sure, ask now!]

   _____

   _____

   _____

4. What can you do now to revise, if necessary?

   My revised showname is:

   _____

Answers:

No answer key from me on this one!

Instead, share your thoughts with me:

Snap me @LaptopLaura on Snapchat

Tweet me @LaptopLaura on Twitter with the hashtag #CopyBook. I want to hear from YOU!

2.3: Not-So-Subtle Subtitles

What is it?

YOU CAN CHOOSE TO include a subtitle in large font size at the top of the page in iTunes next to your artwork.

You may also choose to include it on your website or when you communicate with others about your show, especially if your showname (see Chapter 2.2) is more creative and concise than literal and descriptive.

Here is an example from The Smart Passive Income Podcast.

The part after the colon is his subtitle.

This is not required, as you may see it missing from other shows I have mentioned thus far in this book.

But it is another spot to leverage, and I think Pat does it well.

Let's explore more...

.

Why should podcasters care? Benefits to your brand and business

Similar to your showname, you'll want to be mindful of keywords and catchiness for a few reasons.

Your show will be found more frequently when people search "copywriting tips" (for me, for example) or "online business" (for Pat Flynn, for example) if the subtitle of your show contains those relevant keywords.

Think of a subtitle like the H1 headers in a blog post. The title of your blog is the showname, and once a person wants to look a little deeper, then next thing they'll do is scan your subtitle for more clues about whether or not the podcast is relevant to them and their needs.

But keywords aren't the only important factor.

You still need to craft your copy in a way that entices more viewers to actually click a button to listen to your show.

You'll lose downloads and new listeners if your subtitle is confusing or does not communicate accurately what the show covers.

Laura's experience

How did I craft mine? Well, I started by looking at what other people I respected were doing.

One person who comes to mind is Pat Flynn.

He has a few shows I listen to (so he must be doing something right to have grabbed my attention!) and his personality seems to jive with my own. I consider us both to be down-to-earth teacher types, so I figured his copy would be a good place to start for inspiration.

Once I looked at his Smart Passive Income show (and a few others) and saw how he was leveraging keywords and catchy copy, I wrote up my first draft.

Since then, I have gone back and edited it a few times.

As your show matures, you may find that your direction or focus has also changed. So you will want to reflect that in all writing that is out there about your show, including in the subtitle.

For example, I thought I was going to talk about email list building a lot more than I ended up doing. When I launched my show, I was active in Bryan Harris's Rapid List Building course and private Facebook Group. [Which I highly recommend, by the way.] But as the months progressed, I found that my guests and I were not really addressing that topic head-on, so I removed it from the subtitle.

Again, it's your show. This is okay.

That should relieve a bit of stress you may be feeling about crafting the perfect subtitle. It's not set in stone. It can be improved.

I truly believe that progress is more important than perfection, so give it your best go, move on to the next thing, and circle back after you have more data and experience.

Great examples

Like I mentioned, I looked to Pat Flynn for inspiration. I also checked out Josh and Jill Stanton from Screw the Nine to Five when I first wrote mine, so here are screenshots of theirs!

[Influencer insights from Jill later in this book!]

How to implement this right now

Activity

Now that you have some solid tips and examples in mind, let's get brainstorming.

NOTE:

Even if you already have a subtitle for your podcast, this is still a good exercise. You may come up with something so much better and be compelled to revise. I've done it a few times myself.

Step 1:   Clear your world of distractions.

- put your phone on airplane mode

- silence notifications from your computer

- shut the door and hang a 'do not disturb sign'

Step 2:   Put 3 minutes on a timer.

Step 3:   Put pen to paper or type into a Google Doc, and write out all the words that describe yourself as the host and the topics you discuss on the show. Refer what you wrote from Chapter 2.2's activity on showname creation and I invite you to write in the lines provided below.

_____

_____

_____

_____

Step 4: After doing this for about 3 minutes, it's time to pick a few of the best words and put it together. Look back at examples for inspiration.

Step 5: Put 5 minutes on the timer.

Step 6: Write down the synonyms you hadn't yet considered and play with new combinations.

_____

_____

_____

_____

_____

_____

_____

From this exercise, you're going to produce a lot of creativity and a lot of ideas.

Step 7: Moving forward I would suggest selecting your top 4 or 5 and then taking it back to your tribe, your community online, your friends and family even. Ask for their feedback.

Pop Quiz

1. T / F:

   The subtitle of your show should *only* include your name and the name of your business.

2. T / F:

   The practice of "keyword stuffing" or just including as many keywords as possible -- no matter how it sounds -- is the preferred strategy for writing your subtitle.

3. T / F:

   The most effective subtitles include elements that are attention-grabbing and demonstrate relevance in your niche with the use of keywords.

Answers:

1. F - I suggest using some other relevant keywords.

2. F - This is never true. Do not keyword stuff. Write for humans with the bots in mind.

3. T - Yes. Remember to keep your audience in mind first!

2.4: iTunes Podcast Show Descriptions (also for SoundCloud, Stitcher, iHeartRadio, etc.)

LET'S START WITH ITUNES.

At the time of this writing at the end of 2016, iTunes is the big game in town. If you aren't on iTunes with your podcast, your chances of being found (beyond through your own efforts in social media and on your website) drop significantly.

And let's talk about "being found."

Q: How are you found in Google?

A: When someone types in your name, your business name, or a word or phrase that you rank highly for because you have demonstrated to Google that you legitimately offer great value around that word.

Q: How does Google deem your being valuable?

A: While it is a complex algorithm that I am not going to try to describe here (and no one really knows the full scope...they work hard to keep it that way), what I do know is that, currently, their bots that scavenge the web rely on reading text. Seeing keywords. And, of course, seeing other sites that are reputable and relevant directing traffic back to you too.

Think of iTunes as the Google for podcasters.

Yes, there are other ways to get information online like Bing and Yahoo!.

But none are so big.

And there are other ways to be found with your podcast like SoundCloud, Stitcher, GooglePlay, and iHeartRadio (all of which, I do recommend you share your podcast on - and more!).

But if for now we just focus on iTunes and nailing a great description, we can also copy and paste what we come up with for the other platforms and be off to the races.

Why should podcasters care? Benefits to your brand and business

Like I described above, just being in iTunes exposes you to a whole subset of audience who is actively looking for audio content to listen to, and iTunes is the current major player in that arena.

A well-crafted show description will benefit you in two respects:

1. Get you found more often in search

2. Get more visitors to turn into listeners and subscribers

Combine these and you will get:

- Bigger download numbers for you

- More exposure you can give to your guest

- Greater leverage to attract future guests (and bigger fish!)

- Sponsorship opportunities

- Invitations to be interviewed by other podcasters

- Media features

- Increased authority in your industry

- More subscribers, ratings, and reviews (which ALSO increase your chance of ranking high in the search)

You get the picture! [Remember the tree!]

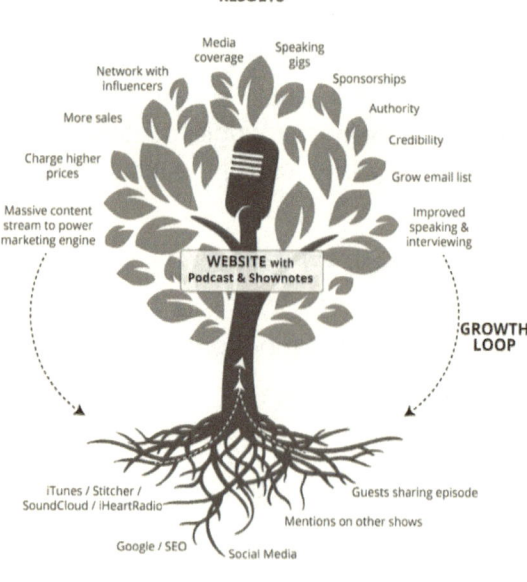

RESULTS

Media coverage · Speaking gigs

Network with influencers · Sponsorships

More sales · Authority

Charge higher prices · Credibility

Massive content stream to power marketing engine · Grow email list · Improved speaking & interviewing

WEBSITE with Podcast & Shownotes

GROWTH LOOP

iTunes / Stitcher / SoundCloud / iHeartRadio · Guests sharing episode

Mentions on other shows

Google / SEO · Social Media

TRAFFIC

Laura's experience

The way I got mine started (and how I coach our clients through it), is a bit of "market research."

The first thing I did was visit some of my favorite podcasts -- regardless of genre -- and see what they were doing.

Then I sought out podcasts who would be 'competitors' of mine (but that is too strong a word -- there is room for us all, and competition is a great sign of market demand).

For both of the above, I read their descriptions and took mental note of how they were crafted and which ones made me want to play an episode and which made me think, "Wow, that is well written."

Then I also looked to see how often they used keywords that would clue in the search engine and visitors that they are indeed relevant for certain topics.

Let's make up an example on the fly of "less effective" and "more effective" to illustrate.

In the form of a Pop Quiz...

Pop Quiz

Read each below and tell me:

Which is less effective and which is more effective?

NOTES:

- *Assume this is a part of a new description for Copy That Pops, my podcast that applies writing tips and Psychology hacks to online entrepreneurs.
- *Keep in mind both reader engagement and keywords for search.

A. Join host Laura Petersen M.A.E.D. as she conducts fascinating interviews with the biggest names in the industry! Her educational background and passion for putting pen to paper in a clever, catchy, and compelling way shines as she asks all the questions you have on your mind to get you performing at your best in your business.

B: Want to attract more readers to your blog? Need more conversions from your email sequences? Wondering why customers aren't buying from your sales page? It's your copy. Laura Petersen and guests share tips, tricks, and tactics to improve your copywriting for more opt-ins and sales in your online business.

What do you say?

[Tweet or snap me your thoughts @LaptopLaura with the hashtag #CopyBook. I want to hear from YOU!]

My thoughts:

A = less effective

B = more effective

Let's analyze.

'A' has some elements of strength. One could argue that putting that I have a Masters in Education with the "M.A.E.D." could be social proof of authority. Words like "fascinating," "biggest," "passion," "clever," and "compelling" are good to pull the reader in.

Q: But what's missing?

A: Reader Buy-in

In 'A,' the wording is more vague around what it is the show actually covers. Someone may read it and think, "Yes, I want to perform at my best in my business....but what exactly is yours? What are you covering?"

Any time someone needs to 'figure it out,' expect a higher bounce rate (a.k.a. people just leaving altogether).

Option 'B' begins with questions that are targeted and specific. It begins immediately with pulling the reader in with a question and getting them to think about their own blog, conversions, and email sequences.

Now the show's ideal audience can see that this show is for them, because these are the very topics they want to improve and see now how copywriting affects their success.

Overall, 'B' is a bit more reader-focused and less host-focused. While you want to prove you are a pro, a well-crafted description of the show can actually lead to more credibility than listing out your degrees and accolades.

What's more, option 'B' also hits those keywords the iTunes algorithm bots are looking for when deciding where you should or should not appear when someone searches.

Say that a podcast listener searches "copywriting"? Which has a better chance to appear?

Did you notice that in 'A,' we never said "copywriting"? Who searches for "put pen to paper"? No one.

'B' is the winner.

Now, as we all know, there are many ways to craft a great description and each of you have your own tone and style. Each industry has its own keywords that are important.

Plus, some good news, you can change and update your show description.

So if you have one that could use improvement, work on that now!

[See activity below.]

Not sure where to start?

Here are a few words of wisdom.

1. Your description should be long enough to explain your show and what it is all about

(being sure to feature relevant keywords), but short enough to keep the reader's attention.

2. Put the most important and compelling part of your podcast at the top in the first few sentences because only a few lines will show before someone has to click "more" to see the rest. You want the best stuff 'above the fold' before someone has to click to see more.

Let's dive a bit deeper.

Great examples

1. Here below is a screenshot from John Lee Dumas's EOFire

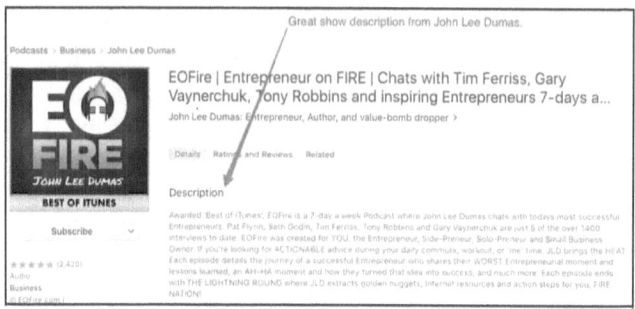

Some things I like:

- Begins with "Awarded 'Best of iTunes'" - umm, hello social proof

- Further social proof with name-dropping big guest interview names (this tactic also helps if people search for these names and find your show)

- Strategic use of ALL CAPS to draw attention to areas and make scanning easier

- Ends with "for you, FIRE NATION!" which alludes to a special tribe that you could be a part of if you listen in

Bonus:

Notice that subtitle. Damn, JLD, you are nailing it. Refer back to Chapter 2.3 for more on subtitle crafting.

2. Here is one from Khierstyn Ross of Crowdfunding Uncut.

Some things I like:

- It's long and detailed so it is hitting on a lot of keywords and there's plenty for someone who wants to learn more before clicking 'play.'

- Although it's long, it keeps you interested and makes you identify with Khierstyn, as you read about how a failure turned into a huge success.

- The style of writing is approachable and realistic. I feel like I could learn a lot and am not going to be sold hype, just real insights into what is and is not working.

- She describes huge benefits that can come from crowdfunding to paint the picture of why it's important to learn more (and listen to the show!).

INSIGHTS FROM AN INFLUENCER: KHIERSTYN ROSS

Speaking of Khierstyn, she was kind enough to weigh in with some words of wisdom from her experience specifically for you in this section!

Bio

Khierstyn Ross is a Crowdfunding Product Launch Strategist who has helped creators raise more than $1.5 million through Kickstarter and Indiegogo.

She is the host of Crowdfunding Uncut, a podcast set to deconstruct what makes a successful Kickstarter campaign.

In her spare time she loves training for an Ironman triathlon, traveling, and enjoying life in Toronto. Find out more at CrowdfundingUncut.com[27].

Insights from Khierstyn about iTunes show descriptions:

When it comes to your podcast, being as specific as possible as to what people will get from your podcast needs to be communicated.

The more specific you are, the easier it's going to be for you to communicate that through your show description in iTunes and other platforms.

---

[27] http://www.crowdfundinguncut.com/

Podcasting is a grind, but you'll be successful if you can give your prospective listeners the tools to find you more easily, that's where iTunes will help you become found.

When it comes to descriptors, be sure to make your iTunes description keyword rich. Show notes are amazing to help someone on Google to find you organically [more on this in Chapter 2.7.

Put it this way - if you do not make yourself easier to find through keyword optimization in iTunes and Google, it will be very hard for new audience to find you.

Your current advertising strategy needs to include not only sharing new episodes with your audience and on social media, but be sure to be searchable!!

For a great example, one of my podcast guests, Nathan Chan of Foundr Magazine, became one of the most downloaded digital magazines by making his product keyword rich in the App Store.

———

Khierstyn is spot on!

Learn from her example and wise words of advice. It will help your show get found and convert more listeners.

How to implement this right now

Activity

Now that you have some practical tips and examples in mind, let's get writing.

NOTE:

Even if you already have a description for your podcast, this is still a good exercise. You may come up with something so much better and be compelled to revise. I've done it a few times.

Step 1:   Clear your world of distractions.
- put your phone on airplane mode
- silence notifications from your computer
- shut the door and hang a 'do not disturb sign'

Step 2:   Put 5 minutes on a timer.

Step 3:   Jot down your top 6 to 9 keywords or phrases you would really want to be found by others when searching in iTunes.

_____   _____   _____

_____   _____   _____

_____   _____   _____

_____   _____   _____

_____   _____   _____

_____   _____   _____

Step 4: Open iTunes. Search your top 3 keywords and phrases above. Browse who shows up at the top. Copy and paste their descriptions here below (or take a screenshot of each):

_____

_____

_____

_____

_____

_____

Step 5: Navigate to your favorite 3 podcasts that you, as a listener, like best (no matter what their industry or show type). Copy and paste their descriptions here below (or take a screenshot of each):

_____

_____

_____

_____

_____

_____

Step 6: Put 5 minutes on the timer.

Step 7: Looking at all the pieces from Steps 3 to 5, write your first draft of your own iTunes description (don't worry if it's not perfect, just write).

_____

_____

_____

_____

_____

_____

_____

Pro Hint:

Remember to put the most compelling and important pieces at the top! And always keep in mind what the audience will care most to hear about (benefits to THEM are usually above all else).

Step 8: Ask for feedback from another podcaster (who has a description you like and who you know hits the targets!) or members of your audience, if you have some.
If you cannot find either, explain what we have talked about in this chapter to someone who is a strong writer and ask him/her to proofread your description and share gut reactions and feedback.

Step 9: Incorporate feedback and new insights into a revised description.

_____

_____

_____

_____

_____

_____

_____

Step 10: If you have a podcast already, update your description with your new and improved one! If you do not have a podcast yet, save this description in a master file along with what you have written for previous chapters so it's all in 1 spot when you need it.

Note: _Use this iTunes description for other platforms too! No need to reinvent the wheel unless you need to shorten what you have to meet a word count limit._

Bonus: Quick call to action

Have a show description that rocks and helps your show grow? I'd love to see it!

Snap me @LaptopLaura on Snapchat

Tweet me @LaptopLaura on Twitter

2.5: Episode Scripting and Guest Question Crafting

What is it?

UNLESS YOUR PODCAST LITERALLY starts and ends with your talking -- 100% stream of consciousness -- you will need to write (or outline) a script at some point for your podcast.

This could include all or some of the following:

1. Pre-Intro

From the voice-over talent along with music at the very start of the show

2. Intro

From you the host to ease listeners into the episode before launching into the meat of the show

3. Meat of the episode

Host's presentation and/or interview of guest

4. Questions for guest

What the host asks and in what order

5. Outro

From the host to wrap up important points mentioned and highlight key takeaways

6. Post-Outro

From voice-over talent along with music at the very end of the show (should include a CTA: Call To Action)

Some podcasters write up everything they plan to say before they say it.

Others only script what the voice-over talent will read to create the intro and out with music on as the bookends of the episode.

Those in the middle may write out bullets of things they want to make sure they mention -- as a guide -- but then speak it however it comes to mind. And they may write out questions to ask the guest.

I'd guess that most of us like to prepare at least a little bit, especially when we are brand new or have a big-name guest coming on.

Wherever you fall, at some point you will be crafting a script or, at the minimum, an outline of where you plan to go during the show.

Writing is involved.

Why should podcasters care? Benefits to your brand and business

As you get more seasoned and experienced, you will likely rely less and less on prepared questions and pre-planned scripts, but in the beginning, it would be a disservice to your audience and show not to put some effort into crafting the best show possible.

Putting your ideas down on paper (or in a Google Doc, like I am doing now as I write this book), helps you get everything bouncing around in your head out.

From there you can organize things.

From there you can clarify weak areas.

From there you can check that nothing important was missed.

This extra effort in the beginning is going to make for a better listening experience for your audience, which will lead to more shares of your show, and more growth.

Remember, this is another key branch feeding into your brand and business. If you want to communicate the impression that you are organized and thoughtful, writing things out ahead of time is a must.

Laura's experience

Personally, I wrote out everything for my first few episodes.

My 000, the "about us" episode was a completely typed out script that I tried to read as if I weren't reading.

Link: http:// copythatpops.com/000

Same goes for 001 which was called "3 Seconds is All You Get: The Psychology of Why Landing Page Optimization Matters." I wrote that entire thing out like a blog post almost and tried to read and perform it to sound natural.

Link: http://copythatpops.com/001

My first interview?

Episode 002 "How Shaunta Grimes went from 0 to 1700 Engaged Subscribers and Earned Enough to Quit Her Job in Just 2 Months." I wrote out all my questions as an anchor. I then tried really hard to "be present" and not just a question-asking robot, but I over-prepared to make sure I would do a good job.

Link: http://copythatpops.com/002

As I got more and more shows under my belt, I pre-wrote and prepared a lot less. I likely sounded more confident too. This is natural. This is normal.

Now I will jot down a few bullets of things I want to be sure to cover, and just "go"!

But that extra effort in the beginning was a part of the process. It's important.

INSIGHTS FROM AN INFLUENCER: JOHN LEE DUMAS

As we saw, in Chapter 2.2's Insights from an Influencer, JLD from EOFire is back!

This time he weighs in on question crafting.

The following transcript is taken from an portion of the audio-recorded session I had with John in late November, 2016.

To listen to the full interview, visit http://copythatpops.com/052.

Laura:

You're known for asking the same questions in each episode, which is a great style. It's not for everyone, but I think it's a great approach.

I wanted to know what was your process for selecting the questions that you do ask.

John:

For me, I knew who my avatar [ideal target listener] was. My avatar was somebody that was driving to work every single day to a job they didn't like, and they had just a very short period of time that was their personal time. That time was probably pretty much during their commute to work.

I wanted to make sure that when they press play on EOFire, that they knew what they were gonna get. They were gonna get me talking for 15 minutes about my weekend or cats or something along those lines.

They knew that we were going to get right into meaningful content during their very limited free time that they had to really be absorbing content from successful entrepreneurs.

For me, I knew what was not being talked about the most, which I thought was really important, was failures and the struggles entrepreneurs face.

Every show that I listened to back in 2012 and before was all focused on the successes and how they're doing great and why they're doing great, and that's all important, and we talk about that on my show as well, but I wanted to start the show off right, in my opinion, by taking the guests down to the level of a lot of the listeners, which was somebody who was scared and struggling and failing over and over again.

I have that 'worst entrepreneur moment' to really set the tone, and then we do move into one of their 'greatest ideas / aha moments' and then we move into the lightning round with like six really hard-hitting questions that extract a lot of great knowledge.

That was how I knew that my listener was going to get the maximum value.

Yes, we ask the same questions on every single show, and they've barely changed in over 1,500 episodes, which just shows you that I really knew who I was speaking with episode 1 all the way to episode 1,500.

But, the key thing with my show that I think people need to realize when they're constructing their format, or lack thereof, is if you are going to have repetitive answers.

The answer for EOFire is: of course not, because we have probably one of the most unique shows out there as far as what the content is every single day because nobody can tell the same worst entrepreneur moment because everybody's had their own, unique entrepreneurial worst moment.

And same with their greatest idea and how that came. So, a lot of the themes to take away are gonna be the same, but every story is different, so we focus on the story.

That keeps it super unique.

Laura:

Right. That makes a lot of sense, and how about re-purposing? Because you ask the questions over and over, is there anything else you can do with those answers that maybe someone couldn't if it were more free-flowing?

John:

Yeah, I think that you could definitely do something like, "The 10 Top Entrepreneurs' Worst Moments." You can have those things because you have those themes that are kind of developing throughout, so there's a lot of things you could do repurposing-wise when you have those kinds of anchor points. A same question is an anchor point. Where if you don't, what are you really comparing yourself against?

To add to this last comment of John's, many podcasters who take the approach of asking the same questions of their guests repurpose and repackage the answers together as lead magnets, bonus content in a membership ship, a book, or other creative uses.

Food for thought!

To look at another approach, let's check-in with our next mega influencer! (Who interviewed John on his 500th podcast episode!) Michael O'Neal returns next.

INSIGHTS FROM AN INFLUENCER: MICHAEL O'NEAL

We also heard from Michael in Chapter 2.2 on Show-Stopping Shownames.

To remind you of his remarkable background again before we hear him ring in with a different point of view on episode scripting and question crafting....

Brag-Worthy Stats

- Hit iTunes Top 10 Business List within the first month of airing
- Nominated as "Best New Show in 2013" by Stitcher Radio
- Named in the "35 Outstanding Podcast Picks for Entrepreneurs Like You" by *INC Magazine*
- Named in the "100 Podcasts That Will Make You Smarter, Better, and Wiser" by *INC Magazine*
- Released over 500 episodes and earned 8 million downloads

Direct Advice

The text below is an excerpt from a conversation that Michael and I had in late November, 2016. It is at http://CopyThatPops.com/051 if you want to hear it in full.

Worth a listen!

And take some notes on this one.

Laura:

...around the episode scripting or question scripting for an episode. What's your process in crafting questions that you're going to ask guests, or maybe how was it in the beginning? Maybe you're so used to it now it just comes naturally, but can you speak a little bit about the questions that you ask guests?

Michael:

This is where my philosophy might be a little bit different. My show is truly such a conversation that I don't typically do that at all; although I just did for Episode 500, which is really interesting. I broke my own format by having some questions that I crafted.

So, I'll tell you what my narrative was and then I'll tell you why.

First and foremost, you have to decide what the narrative of the show is going to be. If you have someone on, let's say that you've got ... I just had this guy, E. Brian Rose, on my show. He's the founder of JVZoo. I know they do affiliate marketing.

That's their main thing is that if somebody wants to try affiliate marketing, there's literally hundreds of thousands of companies that are registered with JVZoo. You can find one and promote their product. That's basically what they do.

Now I would take that data and I wouldn't say, "Okay, how do I become an affiliate?" because that show's been done a million times.

I would say something like, "What are the challenges of becoming an affiliate in a very specific niche, if you don't know anything about the niche?" or something like that. I'll have to define a narrative for the show, and then I would write questions based on that narrative.

Laura:

You're almost coming up with the title as well before you go into-

Michael:

Kind of, at least a concept for it because I want to be able to ... First of all, I want a different take than has been heard on many shows, but I also want one that someone can go, "Okay. These are the shoes that I'm in right now. I'm not really particularly interested in these 5 categories, but they've just demonstrated how someone who's even not interested in the categories can build a business from them." And that's interesting to me.

What I would do then is, as I'm moving through and guiding, I always think of it like a little boat that has one of those little engines in the back and you just steer it.

I may craft a couple of questions ahead of time just because I want to have a theme and get to them. Typically I won't, but I'll start with something and then I'm always active listening and always following up.

So, it's very often that I get to one question and I never get to question number two because it'll go in certain directions, but I'm always guiding it with the rudder if I can, just guiding that narrative with the rudder.

In fact, it's a rookie mistake to not eject from your questions, very much so, because sometimes you can have this beautiful, organic conversation and then someone goes, "Okay. Now it's time for the Tornado Round," or whatever.

We were so good. We were so good. It was getting so good. [Laura laughs]

For my Episode 500, which just aired last Friday, we are speaking in November of 2016, my narrative of the show was I want to timestamp these four iconic guests that I have on the show. I want this date to be timestamped November 17, 2016, because if someone goes back and listens to the show, I want them to know where they were and where they were going. So, my questions are based on that, the narrative of the show was to timestamp.

My questions were, "What have you done in the last year that's been a game-changer for your business?"

Then I also asked some people, "Your life, what's the game-changer in your life? From a business standpoint, what are you not good at?" That was the second question I asked everybody.

I wanted the listeners to see what progress this person has made in the year, then I wanted them to get real. I wanted them to be grounded with my audience. That's why I wanted them to say, "Oh, I'm not good at this." In fact, I learned some things about some of my friends, like, "Oh, I didn't realize you weren't good at that," and that made me connect with them more, right?

Laura:

Mm-hmm (affirmative).

Michael:

Then the third question was about being a beginner because we always feel like we're a beginner. It was, "How often are you trying new things you're terrible at? How good are you at being a beginner? How much patience do you give yourself?" that kind of thing.

And then this was slightly selfish, but it's something I think there's still a lot of white space in the industry, which is, "What's your best methodology for working with assistants?"

For someone like me who's a solopreneur, I have superhero syndrome. I want to just do everything myself.

What can I learn about how to actually interact with people so that I can take some of these things off my plate, right?

Laura:

Mm-hmm (affirmative).

Michael:

"What do you wish you would have done 1 year ago?" What do their regrets look like from a business standpoint? Because we all have them. Again, I wanted them to be very relatable.

Then, "What are you most excited about for 2017?" That was the looking forward questions.

So I looked back, I looked at the present, and then I looked forward. That was the narrative of the show. It was to timestamp it.

Now I don't tell the audience that, but that's how I want them to feel. I want them to feel like, "Wow! I learned a bunch of stuff about these people I've heard interviewed 50 times that I'd never known before."

Now it feels like even if they listen to it a year from now, they're going to go, "Oh, wow! He was talking about looking forward to this and, look, he executed on it. That's how successful people do things." Right?

Laura:

Right. I love that creative thought process that goes into it. You're really crafting the story and trying to make it unique.

Michael:

Yeah, always. That's what makes the show the show.

Laura:

I feel like some people don't recognize that going in. They just think, "I'll turn on the mic and we'll just talk," but if you want it to be really impactful, you need to have some kind of plan going into it.

Michael:

Yeah. I mean, generally, I don't always, but I'm in a different-

Laura:

You're so practiced, yeah.

Michael:

Yeah. This is something I'm very good at now.

Laura:

Right.

Michael:

There's a reason why people hire me to be emcees and stuff because I could just wing it. I'm pretty good at winging it, but I wouldn't say that's the norm, especially in the podcasting world. In fact, the opposite, I think, is true.

I think most people are really bad at podcasting.

Laura:

How so?

Michael:

A high 95%, because no one's paid attention to broadcasting. Everyone just thinks that podcasting is whatever their favorite online marketer guy does - is what they do.

It's like, yeah, they're good online marketers, that doesn't mean they're good podcasters. It doesn't mean they're good broadcasters.

Part of this course that I created called The Art of the Interview is targeting exactly that. It's like, "Let me teach you how to do it for real. Let me teach you what a pro would do in this case." I'm not saying I'm a pro, I'm saying traditionally what media has done in this case and, hopefully, it helps people.

Laura:

Can you give 1 example from that, of something that people commonly do wrong in an interview and how they could fix it?

Michael:

Yeah. God, there's so many. [Laura laughs]

Let's take just the intro. Let's take the intro of someone on a show.

The common modern day podcasting version of it, it reads something like, "Today's guest is Michael O'Neal. Michael was born in Toledo, Ohio. He has a show called The Solopreneur Hour. His 5-year journey, starting with the loss of his parents, with just $14 remaining as bank account, has taken him on a circuitous path to success," blah, blah, blah, blah, blah.

It would literally just go through that thing versus what every pro broadcaster would do.

Every pro broadcaster -- watch Jimmy Fallon or Jay Leno or Johnny Carson, or any pro radio person will say something like, "Our next guest has one of the most popular podcasts on iTunes. Three years and eight million downloads later, his audience feels as if they are proudly unemployable. Ladies and gentleman, Michael O'Neal."

Right? That's how an intro is done.

The test is what are the last two words of any good intro? That's the person's name. You never utter their name before the last two words, because you build them up and you edify them.

The best way to describe what it's supposed to be like is from that scene in 8 Mile with Eminem. Did you ever see 8 Mile?

Laura:

I loved that.

Michael:

With Eminem?

Laura:

Yeah.

Michael:

The last scene of the movie, they're in this rap battle. Eminem has to go first, which is the worst place to go when you're in a rap battle because then the other person just take what you just did and then just destroy you.

So what Eminem does is he destroys himself. He uses all of his inadequacies, all of his shortcomings, and he highlights all of them. By the time the next guy has to go, he's got no ammo. He took all the ammo away from the dude. The guy's got nothing.

A great intro takes the ammo away from the guest.

If a guest walks on a podcast, you know they've done 50 podcasts on the same subject, they have their whole thing they're going to do. They've got their narrative, they've got their shtick that they're going to do on your show, take their shtick away.

He's most well-known ... "Pat Flynn" or whatever, "he's most well-known for losing his job and then he created ... ," blah, blah, blah, tell the guy's story that's on their About page as you're bringing them on because then they're going to be like, "Oh, man. I've got to come up with new material. You mean I actually have to talk and be engaging and share?"

That's what I like to do with mine.

Laura:

That's an interesting angle I didn't think about.

Michael:

Yeah. I think what people don't realize in the podcasting space is that, in most cases, the guest is doing you a huge favor.

Oh, here's another one that I think is a massive faux pas: they don't know when to plug.

People have no idea when to plug a guest.

I did a little poll on one of these Facebook podcast pages. I asked, "How often do you make it to the very end of the show, like 5 minutes or less?"

It was something like 15% of the people made it to the very end of the show, yet when we plug our guests, we do two completely boneheaded moves.

1) We ask them, "Where can people find you?" Every time that happens, I go, "Dude, it's your job, it's not their job. It's your job to tell your audience where people can find them. Literally, by definition, as the host, it's your job."

2) Don't do it at the end of the show, do it at the beginning show, when people are actually listening and paying attention and then do it in the middle of the show when people are listening and paying attention, and then do it at the end of the show.

So, you always plug them beginning, middle, and end.

And people in the podcast world wait until the very, very, very end and this awful question, "Where can people find you?" I want to smack them upside the head because it's just bad pod, just bad hosting.

Laura:

I love that. I'm going to stop that immediately.

Michael:

Yeah. Sorry if you do that.

Laura:

No, well it's good to know that because you just listen to other shows and you model what you see and hear without realizing that's not the best way.

Michael:

Just know that when you're listening to entrepreneurial-based shows, that 95% of them are terrible at it. They're just terrible at being hosts.

You've got to listen to actual people that are good, like Adam Carolla is good. He's a pro. When he brings a guest on his show, the first thing he does is plug them. It's the first word that comes out of his mouth is that he plugs the guest. Then they get into the conversation.

What I like to do is plug them at the beginning, and then if they have a good point, or they drop a value bomb, as Chris Ducker would say, I will say, "Oh, by the way, you guys, make sure you can reach out to them on Twitter" and you have their Twitter stuff handy.

I have all that stuff handy right in front of me. I have all their links and stuff right in front of me before we start recording so that I can plug them throughout the context of the show.

Laura:

Right. That makes sense. You could be like, "Hey, if that totally resonated with you, tweet him right now at ... "

Michael:

Right now! Yeah, because that guest wants to feel like you catered to them and coddled them.

By the time you hit stop and you say, "Thank you so much for doing that," they go, "You know what? That was great. I had a really good time."

Then you can say two things that will help your podcast grow.

Number one, "Hey, would you be willing to share this with your audience?" They'll go, "Yeah, totally."

Then number two, you say, "Do you know anybody else that I could connect with that you might think would be great for the show?"

Those two things happen right then. If you did a good job hosting, you'll get a great referral and you'll get a share.

And those are how your show grows.

Laura:

Brilliant. That's amazing psychology applied exactly how it should be. I love it.

Michael:

Cool.

Michael's advice is invaluable for podcasters! And I love how his approach is different from JLD's, but neither is better or worse. It all depends on your own audience, your own personality, and your own goals.

How to implement this right now

The following is the exact template I used for my show, especially in the beginning.

Now I see how I need to add a "plug the guest!" section along the way!

This screenshot shows just a part of it for episodes 15 and 16 with Tonya Darlington and Marcus Meurer.

I used to start each episode sharing where in the world I was an inviting the audience to engage back (since I was living and traveling in Europe for the first 4 or 5 months of my show).

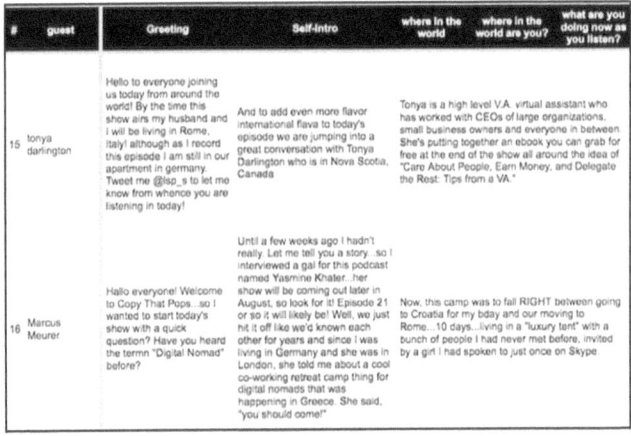

Your turn!

Activity

Step 1: Create a Google Spreadsheet template for your episodes (or steal a blank copy of mine on podcastteachers.com/book-freebies/ called "Podcast Intros and Outros Chart."

Step 2: Make sure the categories on the top of the chart make sense for your show and start writing your intros and outros to fit this pattern.

Remember to think about STORIES like we talked about in Chapter 2.1 and Michael O'Neal stressed earlier in this chapter.

Step 3: Write out types of questions you will ask, or exact questions, during the interview.

Try to craft questions that elicit stories from your guests!

Examples:

- "Tell me about a time when you _____."

- "Can you think of an example when that happened and what you did about it?"

- "How did you transition from ___ to ___?"

- "What did you feel when _____ happened?"

Step 4: Record some episodes using this method. Tweak, edit, adjust, get feedback from your audience. Keep going.

This is a process, not a final destination. You will keep getting better, so go for it.

Fail forward. Learn quickly through action.

Pop Quiz

1. T/F: At some point, most podcasters will script something out.

2. T/F: Give yourself space to tell stories and elicit stories from your guests by crafting your questions accordingly.

3. T/F: Never ask the same question to each guest.

4. T/F: It's best to wait until the very end of the show to plug the guest.

Answers:

1. T - Even if it is just the intro and outro for your voice over guy or gal.

2. T - Stories work on so many levels. Leave space for them.

3. F - This depends on your target audience, your podcast goals, and your own style.

4. F - Beginning, middle, and end!

2.6: Enticing Episode Titles

What is it?

WE ALREADY TALKED ABOUT how to write a name for your podcast as a whole in Chapter 2.2.

But you aren't done crafting creative and compelling names for things.

Each time you publish a podcast episode, it's like putting out a new blog.

And if you link up the audio to shownotes on your website -- which is highly recommended -- you will make use of the title and description again as if it were a blog.

Each episode has its own individual title.

For example, in my episode 036 on Copy That Pops where I interviewed Brandon T. Adams (and got him to reveal things from his past he had never shared before!), I embedded the show's audio on my website inside a blog post.

Personally, I use Pat Flynn's Smart Podcast Player[28].

---

[28] https://smartpodcastplayer.com/

Then I copied and pasted over the exact same title and description that I used when I published the show (via Libsyn) to iTunes, iHeartRadio, Stitcher, and more.

The full episode can be seen here:

http://CopyThatPops.com/036

And a screenshot showing just part of what I describe follows.

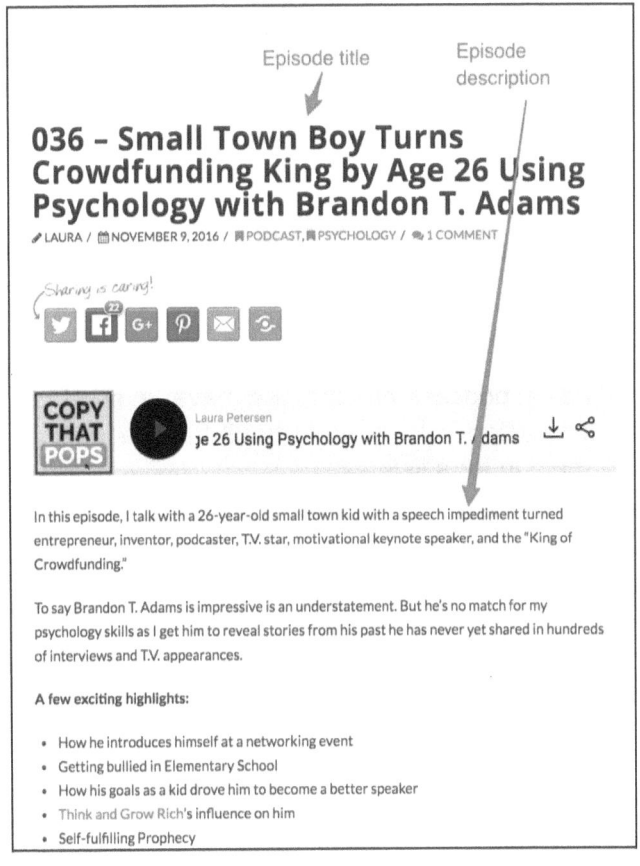

Why should podcasters care? Benefits to your brand and business

Looking at the example with the interview of Brandon T. Adams in the last section, imagine if I had named it:

"Talking with Brandon about Iowa, Crowdfunding, and Psychology"

vs.

"Small Town Boy Turns Crowdfunding King by Age 26 Using Psychology."

Which of the above would you click on?

As an avid podcast listener, I often scroll through different podcast feeds and click to listen and download the episodes that catch my eye and compel me to click.

In fact, 8 out of 10 people only read the title.

As a podcast creator, we have a short set of characters, of words, to hook the reader and pull them in for a listen.

The effectiveness of your titles is directly correlated with the success of your podcast, and thus, brand and business too, since good headlines lead to more listeners, more shares, more awareness, and more sales down the pike.

Laura's experience

Writing great titles/headlines takes practice. There is no works-everytime solution for each person, show, and business.

However, after a lot of research and trial and error, I do have some tips and tricks to help.

Read on!

You are going to hear from an amazing writer who's been growing his blog, podcast, and business for many years even before I caught on to it all!

Then I will share some ways I apply psychology to writing effective titles.

INSIGHTS FROM AN INFLUENCER: YARO STARAK

Bio

Yaro Starak is the Founder of Entrepreneurs-Journey.com and has a long history of creating, managing, and selling successful businesses.

A few include a *Magic: The Gathering* card game trading forum and e-commerce site, a proofreading business called BetterEdit, a blog called Small Business Branding, and a collection of sites about miniature motorcycles.

Yaro created the Entrepreneurs-Journey.com blog and podcast to help entrepreneurs start a blog, grow an email newsletter, and sell their own digital products -- the online business model he has leveraged to make over $1 million.

Since 2005, Yaro has taught thousands of people how to make a full time income using the Blog Sales Funnel[29] to sell digital products and services. You can listen to in-depth graduate blog case studies on his success stories page[30].

---

[29] http://www.theblogsalesfunnel.com/
[30] http://www.entrepreneurs-journey.com/success-stories/

Now, here's advice straight from Yaro

I started my blog in 2005 and my podcast shortly after that (in fact I called it an 'audio blog,' not a podcast - so you can see how I viewed both mediums almost the same).

For me the most important area where writing will dictate how well a podcast performs is the title.

In particular, the title of the blog post where you publish the podcast.

I share all my podcasts via social media and email, and it's the title of each episode that people see first and determines whether they click through to listen.

Hence, I spend the most time on titles (and wow it can be a challenge to come up with succinct yet powerful titles!).

My advice when coming up with titles for your blog posts is to focus on the one big idea or one big achievement that podcast episode focuses on.

I struggle when I try and get more than one idea into a title.

If my guest for a podcast interview did one thing that is really enticing, then I build the title around that.

The other important thing to consider is your audience. What part of the podcast is most interesting to them?

Sometimes the best part of a podcast interview is not the main topic, but something unique or special that came up during the show that perfectly matches the needs of your audience. Audience first!

Good luck with your podcast.

———〜〜———

I support Yaro's advice and encourage you to build time into each podcast episode to craft a compelling title that will be found by search engines and motivate your target audience to click to listen to the episode!

4 ways to leverage psychology to write tantalizing titles

Okay, now here are some thoughts from me for how you can apply psychology to your episode title writing.

1. Visualization and mirror neurons are legit. (Not 'woo-woo' stuff.)

We humans live 'in our heads' a lot. Literally. Let's look at each, in turn.

Visualization

More and more elite athletes and their coaches are tapping into Sports Psychology and harnessing the power of visualizing success on the track, on the field, or in the ring.

Imagining a positive outcome and all the scenarios that could arise help athletes perform better when the time comes to compete.

> *"...the successful golfer knows he must 'see' the ball going in the cup before he strokes it. The good hitter in baseball 'sees' the ball dropping in for a base hit before he swings, and the successful salesman 'sees' the customer buying before he makes the calls."*
>
> ~ Zig Ziglar

Mirror Neurons

Your friend comes in flushed and heart racing. He tells you a harrowing tale about being chased by gunmen and slamming his head into a low-hanging beam as he fled in escape.

As he tells the story, how do you feel?

I bet your heart picks up speed and your head throbs juuuust a little.

In the early 1980's researchers, while studying primates, found that neurons in the brains of macaque monkeys fired not only when they themselves reached for a banana but also  when the watched another monkey reach for a banana.

Those are mirror neurons at work.

What does this all mean?

We are wired to imagine things in our mind. And we even feel what others are feeling as we observe, read about, or hear about things that happen.

No man [or woman] is an island. (Creds to: Poet John Donne, 1624)

We are built to feel empathy and live vicariously through the words and actions of others.

Let's Apply This to Podcast Episode Titles:

A wise and clever technique with your titles then is to get the reader instantly engaged by triggering these principles at work.

Get them visualizing.

Get them putting themselves in the situation. Use words that conjure up images your target audience resonates with and will paint a picture for them.

For example, words "tear-jerking," "shocked," and even "mom" elicit emotion and get us visualizing instantly.

"Shocking tricks for more Linkedin engagement."

"Tear-jerking memories powered him to success."

"Lessons from mom inspired them in 8 powerful ways."

Beginning with action words is another technique like:

"Try not to laugh: Jo Smith shares her worst business mistakes and what she learned."

It's like saying, "Don't picture a pink elephant."

Psychology at work! Get people visualizing and they will be more likely to click to listen and see what your show is all about.

2. Conformity is not just for the spineless.

If you've ever taken a psychology course, you have heard about the Asch Experiment (of 1951).

It goes something like this... imagine you volunteer to participate in an experiment on visual perception. You are ushered into a room with a large table and about 7 chairs. You sit down near the edge of one table where just a seat or two remain.

A researcher in a white coat or business suit enters and reveals lines drawn on the board at the front of the room. It looks something like this:

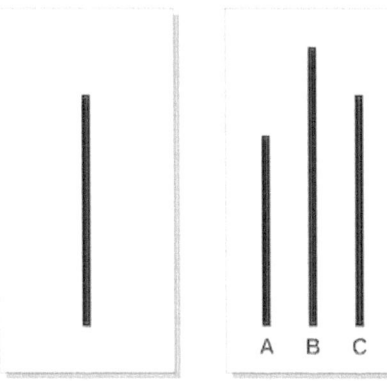

The researcher then explains that they are testing visual acuity and asks each person in the room one by one to identify which line A, B, or C is closest in length to the line at the left.

- Person 1 says: B
- Person 2 says: B
- Person 3 says: B
- Person 4 says: B
- Person 5 says: B
- What do you say?

Turns out, you very likely would say B!

But it's C...duh!

Yep.

But when in a situation like this we often go with the crowd assuming they have more information than we do or that somehow we are mistaken. Or at the very least we report the wrong answer just not to stand out in a 'negative' way.

In this experiment, everyone else in the experiment was actually a 'confederate' who was working with the researcher. The only true participant was you! And they were not testing perception, they were testing to see what you would say.

They were testing conformity.

Read more about the real Asch Experiment at the URL in the footnote[31]. We humans conform at surprisingly higher rates than one would guess. A fact we should all keep in mind in day to day life. But lest I digress again...

Let's Apply This to Show Titles:

Simple. And you already know this. Use social proof!

I have seen websites say things like, "Join thousands of readers and subscribe to our email list." Well, thousands of people can't be wrong, maybe I need to jump on that list!

Or how about, "10 Things Social Media Experts Can't Live Without"?

---

[31] http://www.simplypsychology.org/asch-conformity.html

If you are a social media expert or want to improve your social media, now you gotta read this article to see what all the other 'players' in the industry support.

So for your next episode, maybe your title is, "5 Trends This Fall Competitors Hope You Realize Too Late."

3. Expectations and satisfaction are strongly linked.

Have you ever heard the — kind of true — joke about how the solution to being happier is to 'lower your expectations'?

I know for me that often times when I go into something with certain expectations if they are met, I am happy and content. If they are not meant, I am disappointed and annoyed. Star Wars Episode 1-3, anyone? (the new ones)

Turns out, to a great degree, we like predictability and to know going in what we will find.

Sure, curiosity for what is left missing piques our interest (and could be an entire blog in and of itself), but you better deliver or over-deliver on what you entice me with or you lose credibility and I'll bounce to watch cute cat videos.

Or I'll refuse to watch another George Lucas film, depending on the circumstances.

Let's Apply This to Podcast Episode Titles:

While I am not saying to toss creativity out the window, some of the most effective titles still are 'lists.'

- "Top 10 Social Media Tools: 4 of Which are Free"
- "Sleeping: 5 Ways You Are Doing It Wrong"
- "9 Examples of Effective Titles That Got 3x Increase in Downloads"

By putting numbers in headlines, it gives our brains an anchor for what we can expect.

Then, when listeners hear the information given one-by-one (and see the numbers laid out in a clear list in the shownotes) — delivering on the promise! — they feel pleased and it builds trust.

4. We are all ego-centric.

What is everyone's favorite word ... in any language?

His or her own name, of course!

We can't help it. We see the world through our own eyes and our own perspectives.

Try as we might to fight it, we tend not to fully listen during conversations as we wait for our turn to talk and prepare our counterarguments while the other person wraps up.

We tend to gravitate toward others who look, speak, and act like ourselves or those we are most accustomed to (hence the vital importance of international travel to expand our 'normal' and world view).

We are amazingly kind, generous, and altruistic too! But we do have an ego-centric core.

And for good evolutionary reason.

Think to the caveman days when survival was far harder than it is today with a Starbucks and mega grocery store on every corner. You had to focus on protecting yourself first and your closest kin second, all others be damned. The struggle actually was real.

Let's Apply This to Titles:

Bring your audience in. Use language that gets them not only visualizing but putting themselves into the position of the 'person' speaking or acting.

Using the words "you" and "your" are great for this! Speak to the audience, literally.

Take this study with different headlines for an ecommerce website as a great example:

A: "For sale: Black iPhone4 16GB"
(the regular headline)

B: "Anyone need a new iPhone4?"
(question headline without referencing cues)

C: "Is this your new iPhone4?"
(question headline with self-referencing cues)

Researchers found that:

- question headlines (like B and C) performed better than statement headlines (like A)

- headlines with audience-referencing cues (like C) generated higher click-throughs than others.

NOTE:

This does depend on the message being conveyed as well, so always be sure to test with your own niche and audience[32].

So consider working this into podcast titles. Maybe my next podcast episode will be:

"Is this on *your* top 10 list? Best tools for self-publishing a book in 1 month."

---

[32] http://www.tandfonline.com/doi/full/10.1080/15534510.2013.847859

2.7: Podcast Shownotes for SEO and More

What is it?

SHOWNOTES ARE THE SPECIFIC notes for each episode that you display on your website. What you include in your shownotes is completely up to you and I have seen everything from a few sentence description, to several bullet points, to a detailed blog article summarizing the episode, to a full transcription of the episode (which we address in Chapter 2.8).

No matter how long or in-depth your shownotes are, you must embed your episode to be played by visitors of your audience. Many people discover your podcast upon visiting your website, so you want an easy way for them to play and episode and get hooked. Do not have them "jump off" and go listen elsewhere (like iTunes or Stitcher).

Capture them right there where they are.

So, at a minimum, you need to create a blog post, embed the audio of the episode and copy and paste over the title of your episode. A little more effort -- you will find -- will reap other benefits too.

Why should podcasters care? Benefits to your brand and business

Shownotes do many things. They:

1. Create a place for each episode to live on your website, where it can also be found by web traffic.

Not everyone is on iTunes and other audio playing platforms.

2. Offer your readers a summary or bulleted talking points for them to see if the episode is worthwhile to listen to.

The stealth copywriter in you should craft these bulleted items to sound interesting and get the reader motivated to listen!

3. Allow your visitors to read instead of listen.

Sometimes they are not in a place where they can or want to listen. Sometimes the prefer to read.

4. Improve SEO = Search Engine Optimization.

Like we talked about in previous chapters, current search engine technology relies on robots reading text to measure the relevance of a website (and individual web page) to the keyword.

So, by adding keyword-rich text about your episode on the shownotes, you increase your results in the search engines like Google and others.

NOTE:

This is a long game. Do not expect every episode to be at the top of Google in a few weeks.

But your efforts do compound. The more relevant content you add, the better you will climb the rankings.

5. Link out to things mentioned on the show.

If you are like me, you offer lots of advice that is valuable to your listeners and that includes links to tools, books, and other valuable resources. Make it easy on your listeners to find all the things you mentioned so they can take action on what you shared.

Pro Tip:

Set up an Amazon Affiliates account so anything you mention that can be purchased on Amazon can be your affiliate link. Just make sure to disclose the use of affiliate links on in your website disclaimers. But this can be another source of income as you grow. Check out Smart Passive Income's Pat Flynn[33] to see just how great this can be from sources like Amazon, Audible, BlueHost, and so many more.

---

6. Link out to your and your guest's social media accounts to encourage your audience to engage further.

7. Offer a "content upgrade" or some kind of lead magnet to get your listeners and visitors

---

[33] http://www.smartpassiveincome.com/income-reports/

to subscribe to your email list in exchange for something they will find valuable.

Example: A "Top 5 Tools" checklist relevant to your business niche.

Pro Tip:
You can also use something like LeadDigits from LeadPages to offer a text-to-optin on your podcast. This is where someone texts a word to a number in order to get something in return and you can add them to your email list.

For example, I often say, "Text NETWORK to 44222 to get the links back to the shownotes right in your inbox!"

Even though I announce it audibly on the show, I also write it in the shownotes to remind people.

8. Honor your guest by demonstrating your desire to share their episode and give it its own spot on your website.

This fosters good will and adds value to your guest, which will strengthen your relationship with them. Some of the biggest value you can get from a podcast is from the genuine relationships you forge by interviewing those who come on your show.

Laura's experience

I was lucky in this arena because I got my start in podcasting by helping my great friend (and now business partner at Podtent Marketing[34]) Dominick Sirianni with the show he hosted.

Dom is the co-creator and host of IMA Leader[35], the official podcast of the Internet Marketing Association. A few years ago, he reached out to me and asked for some help on the content side of the podcast.

Knowing that I was a nerd for writing and a growing fan of podcasts, he asked me to listen to each episode he recorded before it went live and write up the shownotes, craft social media messages, and write blog articles inspired by the interviews.

He had already been doing basic shownotes, so I had a solid example to build from.

As I got the hang of it and knew I was delivering on what he wanted, I started tweaking and testing and adding my own flavor and details to them.

You may be thinking, "Nice for you, but I don't have a friend who runs a podcast and wants to share their shownotes templates!"

Well, you have me! :)

I have included a shownotes template you can use (in the Book Freebies![36]) that I created

---

[34] http://podtentmarketing.com/

[35] https://itunes.apple.com/au/podcast/ima-leader-audio-podcast-leadership/id918977514?mt=2

[36] http://www.podcastteachers.com/book-freebies/

building off Dominick's great start and adding my own flavor.

Once you navigate to the Google Doc inside the Book Freebies area, just "Save a copy..." so you can edit it and make it your own.

Feel free to steal this set up and then make it your own. There is no right or wrong way. It depends on your goals and how much time you want to spend making them.

And here is a screenshot of some shownotes from Copy That Pops[37] so you can visualize a finished product.

020 – Landing Pages, Subscription Boxes, and Serial Entrepreneurism – Oh My! with Heidi Koffman

LAURA / AUGUST 16, 2016 / PODCAST / 2 COMMENTS

Sharing is caring!

Laura Petersen

|20 - Landing Pages, Subscription Boxes, and Ser

In this episode, I sit down with Heidi Koffman to talk about her company The Hippie Hobby, lead generation, and marketing automation.

- How she introduces herself at a networking event [2:17]
- Her background and her reason for becoming a flight attendant [3:02]
- How she started The Hippie Hobby [6:32]
- How The Hippie Hobby approaches influencer marketing and lead generation [13:35]
- Her approach to automation with The Hippie Hobby [22:58]
- Why she loves Infusionsoft [32:13]
- How a Lead Magnet tripled one of her businesses [36:53]

Take Action Now!

1. Text NETWORK to 44222 to join our newsletter where you get weekly, short, actionable copy tips!

2. Go to http://thehippiehobby.com and use **PODCAST7** for $7 off your first month

3. Win a Three Month Subscription to The Hippie Hobby

4. Have your question featured on a future show! Below:

---

[37] http://copythatpops.com/020

Let's Get Social:

Guest: Heidi Koffman

Company: The Hippie Hobby

Host: Laura Petersen
podcast@copythatpops.com

All Podcast Episodes:
iTunes
SoundCloud

If you like the show, please leave me a short review on iTunes! It will help it get found by others too.

Sharing is caring!

Gue
Hei
prot
grov

Con
The
craf
fron
com
sust

Quo
"Th

Res
- Infusionsoft
- Parsey
- Cart Hook
- Shopify
- Groove Jar
- Zapier
- ClickFunnels
- Convert Kit
- Canva
- In the Zona

NOTE:

That SpeakPipe (https://www.speakpipe.com/) feature you see in the shownotes was free. It is a way you can get your audience to send you verbal questions or feedback!

Great examples

Here's another example from Elsie and Jess at She Podcasts. They love bulleted lists and so do I!

110 Podcasting Clothes and Hollywood Podcasting News

Overwhelmed with all the to-dos for your podcast production? Team Podcast is here, just for you!?

Support our Patreon page!

Save the Dates: February 23-25 in Florida for the 1st ever She Podcasts EVENT Podfusion via Podfest!

Communicate with us via Twitter by using the hashtag **#AskSheP** and of course follow us on **Twitter**

110 Podcasting Clothes and Hollywood Podcasting ...

30'   00:00:00   ⌐30   🔊   🔽   </>   ☁

Show 110 Super Quick Re-cap!

- Recording from Starbucks!
- Elsie tries not to kill bugs, but let's them outside
- Elsie has a brain-fart...Jess hasn't been gone she's gonna be gone
- Jess gives us the scoop about the Podcast Upfront!
- Jealousy ensues about the awesome keynotes for the upfront
- We discuss the PAIN of leaving your child for doing some work related thing. BLAH.
- What Jess feels about missing her baby's first day of school
- Why it's important for Jess to attend the Podcast Upfront
- Kris from No Extra Words shares her Telebration
- We chat about Derek Halpern and someone using his image ILLEGALLY to advertise their business
- Jess is an awesome interviewer. That is all
- And now we've gotten a chance to know Christy Haussler, the woman behind Team Podcast
- Jenna and Bodhi Elfman are doing a super cool podcast episode for the Wondery!
- Why Elsie loves Hamilton
- StartUp from Gimlet is being made into a pilot for ABC! Woah
- Jess has the coolest opinion about podcasts going Hollywood
- So there's this new contest for podcasts and it's concentrating on podcasts with less than 1000 monthly downloads, which is cool
- OMGoodness John Bukenas is amazing and he has a Diva Package, just for our She Podcasts peeps - email JohnBukenas@audioeditingsolutions.com
- A shirt on Modcloth that was named The Podcast Co-host top in Midnight! We have totally made it!
- We discuss what we're wearing
- And Jess closes with some serious deprecation about going to New York

Links mentioned by Jess and Elsie!

- Leave us feedback via Speakpipe!
- IAB the Podcast Upfront
- Podcast Storyfest
- Derek Halpern, trash seller?
- Wondery Launches First Scripted Podcast 'Secrets, Crimes & Audiotape' (Exclusive)
- ABC Orders Pilot For Sitcom Based On Gimlet Media's 'StartUp' Podcast
- Podster "Best Undiscovered Podcast" Competition
- Podcast Co-Host Top in Midnight by ModCloth
- The Podcast Premier top
- Podcast Party Top
- ModCloth Decrees All Podcast Hosts Must Wear This Flowy, Navy-Blue Blouse
- The Podcast Co-host shirt thread on the She Podcasts group!

She Podcasts thank-you to our community helpers!

- Our editor John from Audio Editing Solutions. He is so good you need to hire him STAT!
- Rebecca Council from CLR Virtual Connections
- Darlene from DarleneVictoria.com

Shop for your podcasting education!

The She Podcasts Shop

Get your FREE How To Podcast tutorial!

Help Us Spread The Word!

It would be stellar if you shared She Podcasts with your fellow women podcasters on twitter. **Click here to tweet some love!**

If this episode got you all fired up, head on over to iTunes and kindly **leave us a rating, a review and subscribe!**

Ways to subscribe to She Podcasts!

- Click here to subscribe via iTunes
- Click here to subscribe via RSS
- You can also subscribe via Stitcher

Feedback + Promotion for Women Podcasters

You can ask your questions, comment below, go to the She Podcasts Facebook group and even share your promos for your podcast! Let your voice be heard. Send it all to feedback@shepodcasts.com

Share This Story, Choose Your Platform!   f   🐦   in   ⏵   G+   𝓟

Related Posts

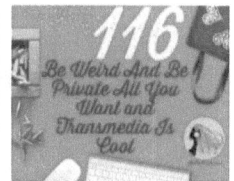

113 Talking, Talking,   117 Should Podcast   116 Be Weird And Be

INSIGHTS FROM AN INFLUENCER: STEPHEN CHRISTOPHER

Bio

Stephen is known for his resilience in business. After being over $100k in debt from a failed mortgage company in 2008, he went on to start two digital marketing firms and won an award for Fastest Growing Company in Colorado.

Today he runs Seequs Digital Marketing[38] and the Business Revolution[39] podcast.

His passion is helping business owners achieve things they never thought possible.

Brag-Worthy Stats

- Had over 25,000 bots love on his podcast interview with me on Copy That Pops with spammy comments (we laugh about this)

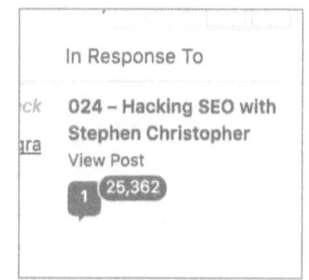

- Won Fastest Growing Company in Colorado twice (1st place one year, 2nd place the next)

- Was the first person to be interviewed twice on Hal Elrod's Achieve Your Goals podcast

---

[38] https://www.seequs.com/
[39] http://bizrevolution.com/

Advice straight from Stephen

You can also listen to this advice on a special mini-series of episodes from book influencers at http://copythatpops.com.

With SEO, I see this happen a lot with podcasters. They don't really know what they're trying to show up for. SEO, searches and optimization is all about what are you relevant for when somebody goes and types in a keyword or key phrase or something into Google, what are you trying to show up for.

A lot of people don't ever actually take the time to figure out what that is that they want to be relevant for in the eyes of a search engine, therefore they basically fail at SEO.

The first step with SEO is to figure out what keywords and what phrases do you want to show up for in a search engine and I would recommend using some sort of a keyword tool because you want to select keywords or key phrases or whatever you want to call it that people are actually searching for, not just something like whatever blue widgets that nobody really searches for. You want to have some phrases that people are actually looking for in search engines because otherwise your SEO efforts are basically worthless.

For example, one of the things that we're starting to go for is 'business podcast' and we're starting to optimize the whole site for that. You're going to be clear about what your keywords are. Tools to figure out what people are searching for, there's

Google Keyword Planner[40]. You have to have an AdWords account but you don't actually have to spend money to get the data. Then another decent one is SEMrush.com. There's a free version where you can get some generic search volume, at least determine if you're going in the right direction with some of your keywords and your key phrases.

Number 1, figure out what keywords that you want to show up for and then make sure that there's actually search volume for that. Be very concise. I would recommend most people with a podcast is going to be pretty specific so maybe 2, 3, 4, maybe 5 keywords. That really, that's it. That's all you want to show up for.

Once you've selected that, now you can be specific through the entire site.

The basics of SEO would be like Metadata which most websites have a field for meta-title, meta-description, etc. [We use the Yoast plugin for SEO in WordPress. And even sites like Wix and BigCommerce have those fields.] That's the stuff that shows up in Google when you search for something. The title is the blue link and the meta description is what's below it 95% of the time. Sometimes Google will pull something else from there but 95% of the time it's what you enter for the meta-data.

Google reads that to determine what a specific page on your site is about. What it's relevant for and then what it should rank it for in a search engine.

---

[40] https://adwords.google.com/KeywordPlanner

Once you've selected your keywords you should go through your site and you start optimizing each individual page for an individual keyword.

Let's just assume you have 5 keywords that you want to show up for; you don't want to put all 5 keywords in every single page of the website. You want to be very clear and concise and specific.

So, let's say you have 5 keywords and you have 5 maybe services that you're offering as a podcast or 5 fields that you can talk about.

You would want to create a page individually for each one of those and optimize that specific page for that 1 keyword. That's going to be the best way to do it.

Yes, the homepage does count as a page so I would pick 1 or 2 main keywords and optimize the homepage for that. All of your other keywords, you want to create individual pages internally within the site and optimize those just for that.

We have meta-data and then we have other basics like alt-tags. That's the actual tag that goes behind an image. For every page of your website including the podcast episodes that you're releasing, you want to make sure that you have as many different media types as possible. You want to have text. You want to have an image. If you have a video, great.

I know a lot of people are recording on Zoom or some other video recording software now, then they're pulling the audio out to make the podcast. If you're recording on something like that, pull out a snippet of the video or even just post the whole video there. Google likes you to have multiple mediums on every single page of the site. Make sure you do too.

Then transcribe your episodes. I actually don't do this, mostly because I'm not trying really hard to optimize Business Revolution for anything quite yet. I have a slightly different plan for that.

But transcribe the episode and in that way that episode will talk about that specific keyword for whatever that episode is that you want to get found over and over again, so that transcription will help Google figure out what content you're trying to show up for.

Shownotes, exactly the same thing. Make sure that you have at least something for shownotes. It doesn't have to be super-long. I don't know, 1 paragraph, maybe 2 paragraphs. Some bullet points. What are people going to learn?

Not only is that great for SEO from a keyword ranking standpoint but it's also from a user experience standpoint.

Google takes into consideration how people are using your website. What's their experience on the website?

If you get a bunch of people coming to the website who are leaving immediately, it's called a bounce rate. They come to 1 page and then don't take any other action and they leave, that's a bounce. The higher the bounce rate you have the less you are going to show up in search results from Google because you have a poor user experience on your website.

You want to give enough content to keep somebody there and have them hopefully interact with your website and that's going to help your rankings too.

Linking. There are 2 forms of linking. Well, there are a couple different forms but we'll talk about 2.

There's internal linking and external linking or linkbacks to your website.

1. Internal linking.

Let's say for example, you have the 5 main services that you offer or the 5 main things that your podcast is about. Anytime you talk about, let's say service or information A, you want to link to information A page on your website.

If you're writing a blog or just airing a podcast that talks about 1 of your services, then you want to make sure to link back to that individual page.

You're really telling Google that, "Hey, service page A is all about service A," and every time you mention service A you link back to that page internally.

Google wants to see these internal links, so don't be afraid to link internally.

2. External linking.

Then we have links that are coming into your website. So as a podcaster, every time you are interviewed on another show you have the opportunity to get a link back to your podcast website.

Make sure that anytime you interview that you go back and check that episode, make sure they link back to your podcast and the more links that you have coming into your website...it is basically like a 'vote' for your website. A vote of confidence for your website in Google's eyes. So the more votes of confidence you have, the more authority you have for a certain subject and then, therefore, the higher you're going to start ranking in search engines for that.

You want to get as many quality links back to your website as you possibly can. If you write guest blogs as well, that would be a great opportunity to get a link back to your website.

Internal and external links, make sure that you're paying attention to those.

Also, they are social signals. So make sure that you're sharing on social. Make sure that you pay attention to what your social posts look like because the more likes and shares you get on social media... that's also a signal to Google that you are now more relevant.

You have more authority on a specific topic and you're going to start to rank a little bit higher. Plus the more you get shared, the more downloads that you are likely to have, so just pay really close attention to social sharing.

Lastly, is create really amazing value. Create great content that is very, very valuable and there will be some natural things that happen for SEO and for sharing.

Just make sure that you're creating massive, massive value.

When I started podcasting I talked to Hal Elrod. I said, "Geez man, what do I talk about? Should I be worried about how many downloads I'm getting and should I be worried about how many shares I'm getting and all that?"

He replied, "Man, just focus on putting out really great content and really caring about the people who are listening and a lot of the other stuff will just fall into place naturally."

And I would say that that's completely true. Just make sure that people are focusing on value and that'll help in the world of SEO too.

I have found the same thing as Stephen shares here.

Focus on creating valuable content first and foremost, then put some thought, time, and effort into earning quality backlinks, setting up relevant internal links, and sharing socially (both from your accounts and also invite the guest to share their episode too), and you are on the path to success.

How to implement this right now

The best advice I can give you in this area, is to grab my Shownotes Template from the Book Freebies page[41] and create one for an episode you have.

As you create yours, you will discover what you like to include and what you'd rather not bother with.

Just keep in mind two things:

1. Who your target audience is.
   Be sure you deliver what will most benefit them and in the way that will best communicate with them.

2. Some of the benefits from shownotes is a long-game.
   Put in some elbow grease now to reap benefits in the long run. High search rankings, social shares, and increased visibility are all at your fingertips.

---

[41] http://www.podcastteachers.com/book-freebies/

Pop Quiz

1. What are shownotes?

_____

2. How are they different from a blog
   article?

_____

3. How are they similar to a blog article?

_____

4. Name 4 reasons shownotes help your
   podcast and business grow.

_____

_____

_____

_____

_____

Answers:

No answer key from me on this one!

Instead, share your thoughts with me:

Snap me @LaptopLaura on Snapchat

Tweet me @LaptopLaura on Twitter with the hashtag #CopyBook. I want to hear from YOU!

2.8: Transcription for Leverage

"TRANSCRIPTION" IS A WRITTEN or printed representation of something (according to Google).

In the podcasting world, when someone talks about transcribing, it is when you take your audio content and turn it into written form, capturing word for word what was said.

Why should podcasters care? Benefits to your brand and business

You may be thinking, "What's the point of going to the trouble to transcribe my podcasts?"

Well, it turns out there are several great uses and benefits.

Let's explore a few.

1. Add the transcription to your shownotes.

(See Chapter 2.7 for more on shownotes.)

This has a couple benefits for both your audience and for you.

For your audience, you are providing them more information in another form of consumption.

Imagine someone who works in an office and does not have his earphones with him. He cannot play your podcast aloud, but he can read the transcript of it.

Imagine a fan of yours visits your website and sees you have a fascinating-looking interview that was just released. She wants to learn from the interview, but she prefers to read over listen to audio. Now she can.

Imagine a listener of your podcast who hears some actionable advice around Facebook Ads but is driving the kids to school and cannot take notes on it. When he gets home, he doesn't want to replay the whole episode to locate the spot where the advice was given.

He wants to just hit "Command + F" (on a Mac) to find "Facebook Ads" in the transcript to zero right in on where the valuable insights were revealed.

In all these cases, having the transcript available gave certain members of your audience the chance to engage with your podcast in a way that better suited them.

For you, like we have talked about already, the more relevant content you have around the topics you want to be known and rank for, the higher you will rank in Google and other search engines.

Transcripts published on your website as a part of your shownotes kick the shownotes up a notch as an uber-content-rich blog article that adds to the inbound marketing strategy you are already implementing.

2. Add the transcription as a separate blog that you link out to from your shownotes

Instead of adding the transcripts to the bottom of your shownotes, you could also add a Call To Action (CTA) at the bottom of your shownotes with something like, "Want to read this interview's transcripts? Click here."

The reasoning behind this could be to getting your audience to go deeper into your website and visit more pages.

It can also give you a chance to optimize both the shownotes and the transcription page for SEO.

Which you choose (1 or 2 on this list) depends on your audience, your goals, and your plan around SEO. I am not an SEO pro, so what I share here are just ideas from what I have seen or tried.

Consult an expert to really maximize your search rankings and see what is best for your website.

3. Offer the transcripts as a lead magnet or content upgrade.

Similarly to #2 on this list, you could include a Call To Action (CTA) at the bottom of your shownotes with something like, "Want to read this interview's transcripts? Click here to get them straight to your inbox."

In this case, however, to get the transcripts the visitor needs to give you their email.

This can be a tool to grow your email list, especially if your interview is with a big industry guru or lots of actionable advice was detailed in the audio.

Check out Chapter 8 for more on this topic!

4. Repurpose the podcast on LinkedIn and Medium to get in front of new audiences.

With the transcript of an episode, you could now write an introductory paragraph and publish the transcript on LinkedIn (as a post) and Medium to get added exposure from people who read from those platforms.

5. Monetize the content.

Package multiple transcripts together and sell that as a book or special edition of the best advice on a certain topic that was covered.

Say you interview 7 Facebook Ad experts over 40 podcast episodes all around marketing and advertising, you could package the transcripts from those 7 interviews and add some worksheet activity to help people implement the advice given. Now you have another product to sell on your website.

Or you could include it as a bonus for joining a membership or coaching program.

Laura's experience

I have dabbled with transcription, but full disclosure, I have not implemented all of the ideas above...yet!

In interview 024 - Hacking SEO with Stephen Christopher[42], Stephen shared some ideas around using transcription services to help him in writing.

He even talked about just recording himself talking out ideas, sending them off to be transcribed, and getting home with the start to a blog article or book chapter just sitting in his inbox ready for editing. That's so much easier than starting to write with a blank screen.

He suggested 2 services:

1. Rev.com ($1 / audio minute and fast turn-around, very accurate)
2. Jennifer Peterson Transcription Services[43] (seasoned pro, contact for very reasonable pricing).

Send an email to one.of.jennifer@gmail.com and mention Copy That Pops podcast for the "Friends and Family" discount.

I then interview Jennifer later in episode 028 - Writing Tips from Transcription Pro, Jennifer Peterson[44], so listen to that episode if you want to learn more about Jennifer and how other entrepreneurs leverage her services.

---

[42] http://copythatpops.com/024
[43] https://audiotoprint.wordpress.com/
[44] http://copythatpops.com/028

Since these interviews, I have used both Rev and Jennifer and included the transcriptions below the shownotesfor about 6 episodes at the time of this writing [check out Stephen's episode 024[45] for an example!].

I plan to get them all caught up to reap the benefits I mentioned above, but it is still a work in progress.

---

[45] http://copythatpops.com/024

INSIGHTS FROM AN INFLUENCER: ANDREW STEVEN

Fun story:

In June of 2016, while my husband and I were living in Southern Germany, I heard of a co-working, co-living retreat taking place in Lemnos, Greece. Lemnos is an island close to Turkey.

I flew out there for the 10 day retreat, never having met a single person. My only interaction was a podcast interview a few weeks before with Yasmine Khater of the Sale Success Show podcast and Earn 5k.

At the camp I got to know a great Aussie who was living in Berlin and running a successful SEO firm. His name is Andrew Steven, or "Andy."

He held a workshop during the camp on SEO tactics and everyone sat riveted. I knew enough from successfully growing my tutoring and test prep company with Todd VanDuzer to know that his advice was spot on and it even included a few things I had not yet tried.

So, naturally, I thought to reach out to him for words of wisdom that podcasters could benefit from to grow their podcasts and businesses using the power of SEO.

Andy's Brag-Worthy Bio Highlights

- Oversaw one of Australia's leading Digital Marketing teams
- 10+ years online marketing experience
- Bachelor's in Advertising and Communications
- Graduate Certification in Business Administration
- Significant experience in display advertising, Google Analytics, ROI tracking, and UI (user interface) optimization
- Adwords qualified

It's his role at High Voltage SEO to discover SEO opportunities to ensure clients achieve their business goals through results-driven campaign initiatives.

Insights Directly from Andy: 6 Simple Steps to Increase the Reach of Your Podcast Through SEO

1) Shortlist 10 keywords you want your podcast to rank for on your website, don't forget to include geographical terms if they are relevant.
[e.g. "San Diego podcast" or "New York Real Estate"]

2) Use the Google Adwords Keyword Planner[46] to discover how many people search these keywords each month.

3) Choose 1-3 keywords that have enough searches to be interesting but not so many as you will never rank for them (say, keywords with 100 - 300 searches per month is a nice place to start).

4) Choose pages on your website to optimize these keywords on. The homepage is always the easiest page on your site to rank if you are only choosing one page.

5) Create 600+ words of content for this page based around your keywords and include your keywords in your:
- Page URL (if not the homepage)
- Title tag
- Meta description
- H1 (you should just have 1 of these)
- H2
- Alt tags (on images)

Wordpress plugins such as Yoast[47] as an aid you in doing this very easily.

6) Promote your podcast through outreach and come up with ways to encourage people to link to your target SEO pages.

That's it! Watch your rankings start to increase.

---

[46] https://adwords.google.com/KeywordPlanner
[47] https://wordpress.org/plugins/wordpress-seo/

So great to hear how some extra effort can pay off. Thanks, Andy!

This is why transcribing your podcast makes sense as a part of this strategy.

You could plan a podcast episode around a keyword and make sure to use it often -- in a relevant context -- and have your episode transcribed. Add the transcription to the shownotes of your episode and optimize in the other spots, as Andy just mentioned!

A few additional ideas for this from Laura to leverage this strategy even further:

- Publish your podcast on YouTube (even if it the audio over your icon) and link back to your shownotes page.

- Write a short "media blurb" hyperlinked back to your shownotes page to offer for guests to use on their pages to show where they have been featured (make sure it shows them off and is not just about your getting a link).

- Turn key takeaways from your episode into a SlideShare, publish it there, and link back to your shownotes.

- Create lots of social share posts and images with linkbacks.

How to implement this right now

Try a transcription service or two and see how you like them. The two I have tried are here again:

1. Rev.com

2. Jennifer Peterson Transcription Services[48]

[Send an email to one.of.jennifer@gmail.com and mention Copy That Pops podcast for the "Friends and Family" discount.]

There are others too, so use what works best for you. But consider how you can use transcription to grow your podcast, business, and brand!

---

[48] https://audiotoprint.wordpress.com/

Pop Quiz

1. What are transcripts?

   _____

   _____

2. Name 3 ways to use transcripts to connect
   with and grow an audience:

   _____

   _____

   _____

Answers:

No answer key from me on this one!

Instead, share your thoughts with me:

Snap me @LaptopLaura on Snapchat

Tweet me @LaptopLaura on Twitter with the hashtag #CopyBook. I want to hear from YOU!

2.9: Lead Magnets and Content Upgrades

A LEAD MAGNET IS something that is super attractive to your audience with the goal of turning a visitor into a lead.

For example, I may share "Top 5 Podcasting Tools Checklist [free]" in exchange for an email address. If it is what my audience wants, then it is a fair trade that people are eager to make.

They enter their email and hit submit, and I give them something in return (usually for free).

How to pull this off?

There are many tools including LeadPages, ClickFunnels, MailChimp, Aweber, ConvertKit, and WordPress Plugins like Beaver Builder.

The technical aspect of setting these up is outside the scope of the book, but do a Google or YouTube search for help and you will find lots out there!

Why should podcasters care? Benefits to your brand and business

Offering lead magnets to your podcast audience does several things:

1. It drives traffic from your podcast back to your website.

If you are offering a product or service, people cannot make a purchase through just your podcast alone.

So your goal should be to drive them to where a transaction has the chance of being made. A lead magnet can be a juicy offer to entice them to do just that and head back to your website.

2. It gets your audience used to engaging with you beyond just listening or reading.

It's like going to coffee when you are online dating. It's a small effort. Low commitment. But it's the first opportunity after viewing the person's profile to see if you want to move to the next level.

As you have likely heard, "People do business with those they know, like, and trust."

Giving someone a valuable 'quick win' on a topic they are interested in builds the know-like-and-trust factor.

If you do a great job here, it opens the door to moving to converting into a purchase (or dinner date, depending on the context ;)).

3. It further reinforcers your 'expert' status in the field.

People need proof that you know what you are talking about before they want to do business. They may have listened to a few podcasts, but a lead magnet can help demonstrate your ability to solve pain points and ability to do it in a clear and interesting manner.

You gain increased credibility by offering some on-point lead magnets.

4. They can help your audience put what was shared on the podcast into practice.

Say that you really took a deep dive into blog writing on a recent podcast.

Why not create a killer lead magnet that is like a worksheet your listeners can download to put each step into practice for their own blog.

Think of it like you are a teacher. Your podcast is your lecture, but students still need a chance to work with the material and apply it to their own lives.

A well-done lead magnet can serve this purpose while also helping you grow your email list.

Pro Tip:

Want to learn more about creative content upgrades and grow your email list with your podcast?

Check out Bryan Harris of VideoFruit[49]. He is the master of thinking outside the box and giving

---

[49] http://videofruit.com/

away "must-have" swipe files for free, in exchange for an email address.

Here's a podcast interview of him and shownotes from Growth Everywhere with Eric Siu[50] that dives into it a bit more!

---

[50] https://growtheverywhere.com/growth-everywhere-interview/email-opt-in-rate-videofruit-bryan-harris/

Laura's experience

I'm a big fan of lead magnets and have a few that I use on my show Copy That Pops.

For example, I have a LeadDigits opt-in, which I described earlier, where listeners can text NETWORK to 44222 to get the shownotes sent to them in an email and be added to the Quick Copy Tip email that goes out each Wednesday.

I have also created episode specific ones that people can access via text or by clicking on links in my shownotes.

For example, a popular one that went with Episode 003[51] was to text FUTURESALES to 44222 or click on the opt-in lead box on my shownotes to get the Future Pacing Worksheet I created that helps people practice the psychology hack I discussed in the episode.

[See following screenshot.]

---

[51] http://copythatpops.com/003

003: Future Pacing – The Simple & Subtle Trick to Get Your Prospect On the Path to "Yes"

✐ LAURA / 🗓 MAY 2, 2016 / 🏴 PODCAST, 🏴 PSYCHOLOGY / 💬 LEAVE A COMMENT

Sharing is caring!

Laura Petersen
Get Your Prospect On the Path to "Yes   003 ⤓ ⤴

In this episode, I talk about future pacing and we dive into why selling the "benefits" of your product is so much more effective than selling the "features."

- What my real estate agent taught me about writing better copy.
- Why helping your audience visualize their future with your product can improve conversions.
- What future pacing can do for your business.
- How to use future pacing in your headlines and landing pages.
- How my business coach used future pacing to get me to work with her.

TAKE ACTION!

1. Homework Mentioned on Show

Text FUTURESALES to 44222 to get #2 below.

2. Future Pacing Worksheet

No matter what you try, remember to keep it short and relevant.

Great lead magnets are not super long ebooks or arduous courses.

Remember that most people are just getting to know you and want a quick win.

Who has the time for a free ebook these days anyhow?

This is not to say that you should never write ebooks! It just means that those belong further down in the customer journey, and I would recommend you charge for them, even if a small amount.

We tend to value more what we pay for.

Plus, it takes WAY less time to create a stellar looking checklist than to write a 30-page ebook. With all that extra time, now you can create 10 lead magnets (instead of one ebook) and display them throughout your website and mention them on different podcast episodes to test and see which most resonate with your audience.

That insight can then inform your decision on what paid ebook or course to develop as a product to sell. The data you can collect from which lead magnets work and which do not is incredibly valuable to you.

It can also give you huge clues around what topics you need to do more podcast episodes on.

Great examples

So I likely convinced you that lead magnets are a good idea, but you still need to know how to make a good one and what a great one looks like.

Here is one I made using Canva[52] (for free) and exporting as a PDF.

Future Pacing

Practice Worksheet - Get Your Visitors Visualizing Happy Results With You!

Change each item below to help your readers VISUALIZE their future with BENEFITS from your product or service! -- Then do it for real and share your results!

Example answer ideas on next page if you get stuck!

1. Self-publish your book online.

2. Request a free demo to see it in action.

3. 50 Proven Headline Formulas

4. Free guide to show you the best money-saving sources

5. Write a line from one of yours! _____

Get More Conversion Help

Yep. I'm a button! :)

Copy That Pops!

---

[52] https://www.canva.com/

Future Pacing
Practice Worksheet - Get Your Visitors Visualizing Happy Results With You!

Some answer examples! There are many ideas that are correct!

1. Self-publish your book online.
   Get your autographing pen ready.

Example answer ideas. What did you come up with?

2. Request a free demo to see it in action.
   Watch a 5-minute video showing how you will increase your sales instantly.

3. 50 Proven Headline Formulas
   50 Proven Headline Formulas [Warning: Unusually high sales volume in your future]

4. Free guide to show you the best money-saving sources
   This [free] guide officially makes you a money-saving maven.

5. Write a line from one of yours! _____
   I'd love to see what you come up with! - Laura@copythatpops.com

Get More Conversion Help

Yep. I'm a button!)

Copy That Pops!

Note that it is short and sweet. It is 2 pages because the second page gives example answers. But this is something that people can use to quickly apply the Future Pacing technique we went over in the podcast episode.

Win-win.

Pro tip:

Although I am handy in Photoshop and Illustrator, I actually prefer Canva.com for creating these. Once I set up one looking how I want with the branding colors and fonts, I just hit duplicate and change the content for a second one.

This consistency in branding contributes to the know-like-and-trust factor. Plus it makes it easy on myself or virtual assistant I hire to help create them.

INSIGHTS FROM AN INFLUENCER: JILL STANTON

I have been a long-time fan of Jill and her husband Josh's website for Screw the Nine to Five[53] and Facebook group[54]. I even told my web designer to look at their page for inspiration when putting together Copy That Pops[55].

So, I was happy when she agreed to share some words of wisdom on lead magnets. She's a masterful pro!

Bio

Jill Stanton is the Co-founder of Screw the Nine to Five—where she and her husband Josh teach unsatisfied webpreneurs how to eliminate the overwhelm, focus on the right tasks, and build their businesses strategically.

She's got an inappropriate love for trashy TV, has the mouth of a sailor, and isn't afraid of a tall glass of gin.

Insights straight from Jill Stanton

Want to hear the audio version of Jill's advice? Check out Copy That Pops.[56]

[53] http://screwtheninetofive.com/
[54] https://www.facebook.com/groups/500493680082315/
[55] http://copythatpops.com/
[56] http://copythatpops.com/049

When you're creating your podcast episodes, I think it's incredibly important to keep your topics 'on purpose.'

What I mean by that is you always want to create really purposeful content that leads the listener, reader, or viewer through either a sales funnel or just a basic sequence that leads them towards getting on your list or making a purchase.

The best way we've discovered to do this is to create very hyper specific funnels. For podcasters this would look like creating an episode around a particular topic, then having a hyper specific, relevant next step lead magnet.

For using our own funnels as an example, I have a sales funnel on sales funnels. So meta, I know.

This is how that breaks down...

We start exactly like what we do with Addicted [their Facebook Ads Course with Amanda Bond - Laura recommends].

Start with a 'read magnet.' [a detailed, high-value blog post]

My read magnet in this case is "How to Create a Dangerously Effective Automated Sales Funnel."[57]

The lead magnet for that is to "steal the emails that I use in my sales funnels." [Jill sends you her actual emails if you opt-in with your email. Genius!]

Then the intro offer, which is the next step of the sequence, is to grab our course The Perfect

---

[57] http://screwtheninetofive.com/how-to-create-a-sales-funnel/

Sales Funnel, and then the final step is to join Screw U [their membership site].

If you're a podcaster, the trick here is to identify what the main interest areas, pain points, or the spots where people really struggle are. The challenges.

Identify what those are and start creating purposeful podcasts around those topics.

Create these next-step lead magnets that are really no brainers because they're fluid, they're hyper specific to that particular episode, and they serve as an automatic 'yes.'

Then have something that is relevant to both of those -- the podcast episode and the lead magnet -- that serves as a next step and helps to change the relationship from listener to customer.

That's really what you want to do with this purposeful content.

You don't just want to create content for the sake of creating content. Be purposeful with it and make it lead somewhere.

Whether that's getting on your email list or becoming a customer of yours or upgrading into your core offer, the key is to stay on purpose and stay strategic so that you're not just falling into the trap of creating content for the sake of creating content.

This advice from Jill is spot on!

I am a big nerd for effective copy and a smart, strategic approach to online marketing, so for my money, Jill (and her hubby Josh) at Screw the Nine to Five are ones to watch.

Follow these wise words and check out her blog[58] and Facebook community[59] for even more.

---

[58] http://screwtheninetofive.com/blog/
[59] https://www.facebook.com/groups/500493680082315/

How to implement this right now

Step 1: Visit some of your favorite websites where the business owners are leveraging lead magnets.

Not sure of any?

Lookup Bryan Harris, Screw the Nine to Five, and Neil Patel.

Step 2: Create a free Canva.com account and select the dimensions for what you want your lead magnet to be. (U.S. Letter is the standard 8.5"x11")

Step 3: Create your first lead magnet!

It's not as hard as you think, especially if you know your target audience well.

- Think about frequently asked questions.
- Or think about the top 5 pieces of advice you would give someone new to your field.
- Or look at your competitors and see what they are doing for inspiration (don't copy it, but it can stimulate some ideas)

Step 4: Title your lead magnet with something catchy.

A few great recipes include:

1. The Top [number] of/that [things your audience cares about] to [get a desired result] in [surprisingly short amount of time]

E.g. "The Top 3 Tools That Increase Your Instagram Followers in 5 Minutes a Day"

2. Step-by-Step Checklist to Get [desirable results] Without [doing something undesirable]

E.g. "Step-by-Step Checklist to Get Booked on Podcast Interviews Without Paying a Dime"

What is the title of your lead magnet?

_____

_____

Step 5: Fill in your lead magnet with great content that you know. Remember to keep it clean, legible, and easy to scan and 'digest.' Avoid millions of font changes and sporadic colors. When in doubt, simple is better.

Step 6: Save it as a PDF to your computer and connect it up with your email delivery platform and embed the opt-in in your shownotes.

You can also create a text-to-opt-in with services like LeadPages, ClickFunnels, and others.

Pop Quiz

1. What is a lead magnet?

   _____

2. T / F: The best kind of lead magnet is long and detailed, such as a 30 page ebook.

3. Name 3 benefits to your podcast and business with lead magnets.

   _____

   _____

   _____

4. What is one tip you would give to someone about how to write a good title for a captivating lead magnet?

   _____

Answers:

1. An attractive give-away in exchange for an email address (usually free)

2. F

3. Varies

4. Varies

For #3 and #4, share your thoughts with me:

Snap me @LaptopLaura on Snapchat

Tweet me @LaptopLaura on Twitter with the hashtag #CopyBook. I want to hear from YOU!

2.10: Social Media - Profiles and Posts

What is it?

WHEN YOU THINK ABOUT your social media profile, you probably think mostly about your photos, your friends, and maybe even videos you share.

Maybe you threw in a few words haphazardly when setting up your profile when it asked for a description. Take a look at your Twitter, Facebook, Instagram, Linkedin, and Pinterest pages.

But the description area of your social media profiles is a great spot to apply some of the same writing skills and approaches we've been learning in other chapters.

The way you describe yourself affects how people perceive you online!

Why should podcasters care? Benefits to your brand and business

The way you describe yourself and your business and your description is a key component of a successful social media profile.

It's your chance to quickly and succinctly tell the world what you're all about and capture their attention so they want to learn more and engage with you further.

Relevant keywords help you get found and let a new viewer know instantly they are in the right place to connect with an influencer (you!) around that topic.

But that's not all.

Social media profiles turn up in Google searches as well.

Getting your description right can improve your organic search results even outside of the social media platform.

Let's look at an example.

When I search my name "Laura Petersen," the first results that are of me (there's another Laura Petersen who is a brunette model), are my Twitter and Google+ accounts.

[See image that follows.]

https://www.google.com/search?q=laura+petersen&oq=laura+petersen&aqs=.

Laura Petersen - IMDb
www.imdb.com/name/nm5773530/
Laura Petersen, Actress: The Dead Room. Laura Petersen is an actress, known for The Dead Room (2015) and Shopping (2013).

Laura Petersen - IMDb
www.imdb.com/name/nm1785554/
Laura Petersen, Production Manager: The Troop. Laura Petersen was born on April 14, 1978 in Chicago, Illinois, USA. She is a production manager and ...

Laura Petersen
www.laurapetersen.com/
Beauty · Body · Editorial · Lifestyle/Commercial · Video · Contact. - Main Menu -, Beauty · Body · Editorial · Lifestyle/Commercial · Video · Contact. x Close.

Laura Petersen Music | Facebook
https://www.facebook.com/laurapetersenmusic/
Genre: Acoustic/Folk/Rock ... Laura Petersen Music, Milwaukee, Wisconsin. 416 likes ... See more of Laura Petersen Music by logging into Facebook. Message ...

Laura Petersen Profiles | Facebook
https://www.facebook.com/public/Laura-Petersen
View the profiles of people named Laura Petersen. Join Facebook to connect with Laura Petersen and others you may know. Facebook gives people the power.

Laura Petersen
www.laura-petersen.com/
Laura Petersen is a science writer who covers the environment, wildlife, ecology and oceanography. Petersen has been documenting the community around her ...

Laura Petersen (@lsp_s) | Twitter
https://twitter.com/lsp_s?lang=en
The latest Tweets from Laura Petersen (@lsp_s). Tall psych teacher turned entrepreneur. Love biz, travel, 4HWW, I.T. Crowd. Never too much garlic.

It's live! www.copythatpops.com/016-02 My first in-person # podcast ...
https://plus.google.com/115729915283339998283/posts/jX1JuNaHptp
Laura Petersen
Jul 20, 2016 - It's live! www.copythatpops.com/016-02. My first in-person # podcast interview (episode #16) was conducted on-location in Lemnos, Greece with Marcus ...

Really <3 this interview with CEO of Double Forte Lee Caraher. Great ...
https://plus.google.com/115729915283339998283/posts/hj5aEaJLtuq

Not me, but they are high-ranking social profiles.

Me

And even the results from the other Laura Petersen show Facebook profiles high on the list on the front page!

Well-crafted copy hooks the visitor and makes them want to read your posts, comment and share on your podcasts, and jump into the funnel from visitor, to subscriber, to customer, to raving fan.

As a podcaster, you're going to be promoting your episodes and your guests, so you want to have strong social media profiles in order to gain more followers, encourage more shares, and ultimately grow your podcast and business.

Laura's experience

For me, my profile descriptions are ever-evolving. I add, delete, and reword them occasionally to reflect what I am currently working on most passionately. They can always be edited!

I try to do to hit both elements that we want of:

- keywords
- catchiness

By making my description:

1. Brief

Keep them as short as possible, while still saying what you need to say.

2. Professional and accurate

Describe what you do and who you are business-wise.

3. Exciting and real

Describe what you do and who you are personally!

Remember that people connect with people around emotion. If you feel strongly about something, whether that is cats, or coffee, or snorkeling in Bali, share it!

Others who feel the same will connect with you. And even those who do not have the same preferences, will see that you are a more dimensioned person than a stiff resume-like description could convey.

4. Searchable with a few hashtags

You can use a few hashtags that tie in with #2 and #3 above to help.

5. Sharing accolades

Have a few noteworthy accomplishments? Feature them.

Great examples

I love Jay Wong's Twitter profile because he features his podcast and shouts out a major accomplishment.

#1 in Self-Improvement in iTunes is awesome! Go, Jay!

Then he also shares his passion and mission with, "Dedicated to purpose-driven humans and passionate creators."

The #changemakers is a unique hashtag that is relevant to his podcast and his niche.

INSIGHTS FROM AN INFLUENCER: MELISSA SUE TUCKER

Bio

Melissa Sue Tucker is a podcaster, public speaker, and addiction advocate. She is in pre-production with a T.V. show with OCW Productions, a contributing author in a Mental Health Awareness book, and also my partner in crime at PodcastTeachers.com.

She has a special knack for finding what works with social media for herself and clients -- and we even recorded a podcast interview together called Podcast Therapy and Instagram[60] that is worth checking out.

In addition to teaching and coaching clients to start their own podcast, Melissa has two of her own: 60 Seconds of Solitude[61] and Addiction Support Podcast[62].

---

[60] http://copythatpops.com/006
[61] https://itunes.apple.com/us/podcast/meditation-podcast-60-seconds/id1079223759?mt=2
[62] https://itunes.apple.com/us/podcast/addiction-support-podcast/id1061223413?mt=2

Insights Straight from Melissa

I am not a writer. This is why I podcast.

I was diagnosed with ADHD in 2011. (Seriously, can you name one entrepreneur who doesn't have ADHD?)

[Laura chimes in with, "I don't! ;-)]

I have a very hard time reading if I'm not totally engrossed in what the author is saying or teaching. Because of this, I keep my writing as concise and bulleted as possible. I like to ask myself "for the sake of what?"

Then I make sure I'm answering that question with my writing.

One area that I've had huge results with is my copy on social media bios:

1. Bios are important - make sure you take the time to fill them out

2. Keep them sweet, simple, and clear

3. Link where you can

4. Use keywords

Facebook:

One of my biggest surprises came when I updated my personal Facebook profile picture.

Here's what I put in the description attached to my photo:

Melissa Tucker
March 5 · Edited · 🌐 ▾

I'm a podcaster! 💜 60SecondsOfSolitude.com and AddictionSupportPodcast.com - Please listen and share! 😄

When I posted it, I wanted my friends to tell other people about my podcasts. I had no idea that people would actually share my profile picture on their page!

Can you imagine seeing YOUR profile picture show up in your news feed because your friends shared it!?!?

It still makes me laugh because a Facebook profile picture (at least on 3/5/16) shows up much larger in the news feed than other images.

I saw a spike in downloads for both of my podcasts within a week or so of posting this.

Here you can see the peaks in March 2016 for 60 Seconds of Solitude:

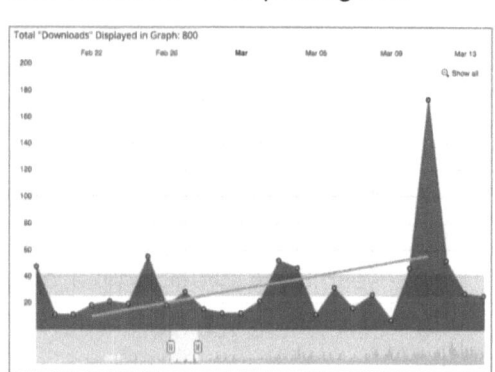

Here you can see the peaks in March 2016 for Addiction Support Podcast:

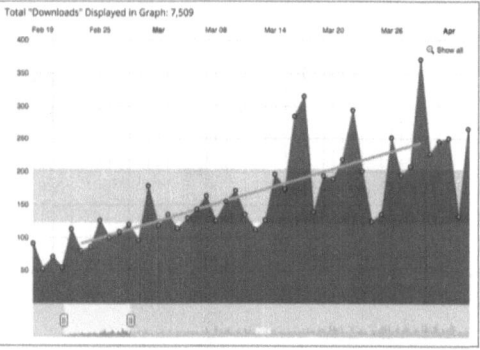

Twitter:

My Twitter profile has helped too!

It's pretty basic but it caught the eye of a fabulous lady who reached out and wanted to know if I would like to have one of the Founders of Facing Addiction on as a guest.

I was so honored because I had just watched The Anonymous People, a documentary that Facing Addiction had created.

Of course, I jumped on that opportunity and not only created an inspiring podcast episode, I also created a relationship with someone who said I could reach out if I ever needed anything.

Just image if I hadn't taken the time to complete my Twitter profile.

My advice on a Twitter profile is keep it short, clear, and include short links.

Instagram:

Now you know I'm going to say to complete your Instagram bio! :) You can have a little more fun with Instagram. People who are on there will only go look at your profile if they want to know more about you.

Here, you want to include keywords in your name and bio. For example, if you follow me @60secondsofsolitude[63] you'll see my "Name" is actually Meditation... because I wanted to come up if someone searched for meditation.

---

[63] https://www.instagram.com/60secondsofsolitude/

I followed Brandon Gaille's advice for setting up my bio. You can find that blog post linked here[64].

All Platforms

My last bit of advice on writing copy - especially on social media - is to be real. Be authentic. People will respond.

When I first started on Instagram, I did not want to alienate anyone. I was scared that people might think I was too woo-woo, or preachy.

But I found when I pushed through that and really started to share my essence, people got it. They started commenting more than normal.

Go for it, push past what you are comfortable with.

Be unapologetically you.

———

Thank you, Melissa, for being so open as to show real data from your own shows and insights from your own experience. You continue to encourage and inspire me, so I am sure the readers will feel the same!

---

[64] http://brandongaille.com/an-instagram-growth-hacking-strategy-that-delivers-targeted-followers/

How to implement this right now

Step 1:   Open up the profiles of influencers you respect inside and outside your industry for inspiration. Screenshot ones that make you want to click and engage with the person further.

Step 2:   Close all windows on your computer (other than any samples for ideas). Then open up all your social media profiles you want to improve and align:

- Facebook (personal)
- Facebook (business)
- Twitter
- Instagram
- Google+
- LinkedIn (this one requires more work!)
- Pinterest
- YouTube
- Anywhere else you need a short, catchy bio

Step 3:   Open up a Word Document or Google Doc and, while looking at what you already have and your samples from others, write a new version of a profile description in general. If it helps, write in bullets first before putting it together.

For example, list out:

- 3 words to describe your work / profession / business
- 2 words to describe you personally
- 2 hobbies or passions
- 1 off-the-wall funny thing about you

Sample could be:

Tall teacher turned copywriting, podcasting entrepreneur. Loves salsa dancing while traveling the world. Huge fan of garlic. PodcastTeachers.com

Step 4: One by one, update your profile description with as close to the same for each as you can (for branding consistency). Some allow more characters than others, so this could be impossible unless you opt for a really short description.

2.11: Social Media - Authentic Growth

What is it?

WE ALL KNOW WHAT social media is.

But I want to talk about the benefits of using it like a normal person instead of trying too hard to hack and automate.

Especially when you are just growing your podcast and business, you have to do things that don't scale so that you can scale (later).

So, I wanted to take a quick chapter to talk about growing your podcast, brand, and business one person at a time, one comment at a time. Authentically.

This may be heresy in the online marketing world, but suspend your disbelief for a moment, if you would!

Why should podcasters care? Benefits to your brand and business

Podcasting is a unique medium of communicating with an audience.

Melissa Sue Tucker pointed out that, "Your voice is literally inside someone's head!" The listener may be multi-tasking as they listen, but there is no other auditory input other than you and your show.

To have a successful podcast (and business) these days you need to niche down, especially in the beginning.

For example, I know a girl named June [names have been changed to protect the innocent ;)] who wants to grow her consulting business on digital marketing.

She quickly found that that space is crowded. It's a good sign that it's a popular topic, but the biggest voices and brands out there are winning the lion's share of the traffic and attention.

She felt invisible.

She felt like even though she had a lot to offer, she'd never get the chance.

But what I told her when she wanted to brainstorm is that where the big fish cannot compete with her is if she niches way down and really focuses and specializes in one area.

For example:

- Using Facebook Live to Drive Prospects to Webinars

- How to Grow Instagram for Custom Jewelry Designers Who Sell on Etsy and Shopify Shops
- Optimizing the On-Page SEO of Blog Articles
- Pinterest for Millennial Mompreneurs

After naming a few of these she loved a couple of them and immediately started rattling off all the ways she could help someone in the small niches.

Like June, if you are willing and able to get granular like one of the above, you can really carve out a name for yourself and find raving fans for the value you are able to provide to this smaller segment of the market.

But don't worry.

As you grow, you can broaden your specialities and services. But you'll be doing it with direct client feedback instead of guessing and instead of trying to be everything to everyone from the beginning -- a losing game.

So let's circle back to the concept of "growing your podcast" one Facebook comment at a time.

Have you ever read Kevin Kelly's 1,000 True Fans[65]? It's a couple minute read and well worth it.

To be successful and earn what we want to earn, we do not need to get as any raving fans as we are lead to believe. We don't need 1 million followers. We don't need our video to go viral.

---

[65] http://kk.org/thetechnium/1000-true-fans/

Sometimes I know I get caught up in the frenzy of as Amanda Bond, owner of The Ad Strategist, would call it "vanity metrics."

- How many likes did that photo get?
- How many comments are on my blog post?
- How many new Twitter followers do I have?

While these metrics *could* correlate with true business success, they are not causational. I can get 1,000,000 likes on a photo, but if I don't have the right thing to sell to the right person visiting, those likes are worth a whopping $0.

So take a breath for a second. Realize that social media is a tool to connect with people, offer value, get paid in return, and grow.

Imagine if you went to an in-person networking event and just ran around the room asking people to give you a high-five or thumbs-up after looking at your product.

No one bought it, but you got 300 high-fives. Greeeeaat.

What if instead of running around the room looking for "vanity metrics" you had taken the time to have a meaningful conversation with just a couple of people who you connected with and felt you could help?

I'll take 1 sale out of 3 conversations over 0 sales out of 300 any day.

Plus, which group of people is most likely to remember you after the party and feel confident it referring you to their friends and business contacts?

Keep this analogy between real life and online in mind.

Popping into Facebook groups to spam everyone with your amazing offer and disappear until the next pitch? - Stop that.

Talking to someone online JUST so you can pitch them the second the conversation turns to you? - Yuck.

Only helping people when you want something back in return? - Nope, not that either.

Stop thinking of "social media" as something different. It's just a digital version of communication mirroring the offline world.

Laura's experience

I'm not perfect, trust me. During the writing and launch of this book I felt a bit icky promoting it all the time.

But for those who know me, and have interacted with me beyond the past month during this mad dash, know that I'm a real person trying to help.

And good karma comes around in some form or another without keeping score on each interaction.

In fact, I've been meeting with the same two mastermind buddies for about 10 months at the time of this writing.

Melissa lives in Arizona (you met her in the last chapter), Tom lives in New Jersey (with plans to move to Thailand!), and I was in Germany when we met.

It was all through the power of being genuine with interactions on Facebook and now we have growing business deals together. My relationships with each of them started with one Facebook comment.

Great examples

For this section, I want you to seek them out. They aren't hard to find.

Jump into your favorite 3 Facebook groups right now (and if you aren't in any, request to add 3 around podcasting, entrepreneurism, and/or your niche).

My favorites are:

- Smart Passive Income Community[66]
- She Podcasts[67] (ladies only, sorry fellas!)
- Screw the Nine to Five[68]

Look inside the groups and just watch the activity for a few days.

Look at who is offering great answers to problems.

Look at who is pitching and running.

Look at who is asking thoughtful questions and starting a discussion on an interesting topic.

Then think about who you want to emulate.

The growth results for you podcast and business will follow.

---

[66] https://www.facebook.com/groups/spicommunity
[67] https://www.facebook.com/groups/shepodcasts
[68] https://www.facebook.com/groups/500493680082315/

INSIGHTS FROM AN INFLUENCER: JARED EASLEY

Bio

Jared Easley is a genuine entrepreneur, podcaster, author, and Co-founder of Podcast Movement, the World's Largest International Podcasting-Only Conference.

He has been called the Zig Ziglar of the podcasting world.

Jared is a noticer, motivator, friend, and power content creator who has found a way to do it all and still keep his family first.

Some Other Brag-Worthy Stats

- Co-Founder of the Academy of Podcaster Awards
- Host of Starve the Doubts[69]
- President at PodMov University[70]
- Best-Selling Author of: *Podcasting Good to Great: How to Grow Your Audience Through Collaboration*
- Named #1 Emerging Entrepreneurial Podcast via Entrepreneur.com and Huffington Post

---

[69] http://www.starvethedoubts.com/
[70] http://www.podmov.com/

Insights directly from Jared:

If you want your podcast to get noticed then you have to start by noticing others first. No one will notice when you are by yourself posting "listen to my podcast." People will notice if you have an army saying, "We love Laura's podcast."

How do you build an army?

Who is your target listener?

Imagine what would happen if you took initiative to authentically (non-schemingly) find ways to notice your target listeners.

It could be as simple as commenting on their Facebook posts, sharing their blog and tagging them on twitter, or even an old fashioned handwritten note of legit appreciation.

Noticing your target listeners in this manner will create rapport. Rapport over a period of time will create reciprocity.

If Laura has noticed me over time then I am likely to begin saying... "I like Laura. She is a really nice person. I appreciate her and what she is up to. I should check out what she is doing."

If Laura comes to me and says "please check out my podcast" or "I have a new book out and was wondering if you would be willing to help me get the word out"... What do you think I am going to say to Laura? I will want to support her. I will want to tell my friends about her and what she is up to because I trust her. I trust what she is doing.

Imagine if this strategy was compounded over time.

5 people turn into 10 people.

10 people turn into 20 people.

20 turn into 40.

40 turn into 80, etc.

Eventually an army of people are saying, "We love Laura!"

When that happens... others begin to take notice. After all, if that many people say they love and appreciate Laura... she must be doing something noteworthy. This is how you build the army.

Start by noticing.

Build rapport.

Rapport yields reciprocity.

I love this advice from Jared. We online entrepreneurs are barraged each day with webinars about high-converting funnels and explosive email list growth.

Those are great. But we have to remember that people do business with people. So, act like a real human and your credibility and business will grow organically, and in a way you can be proud of.

How to implement this right now

Step 1:   Open up a Google Doc or grab a sheet of paper. On the left side, write down all the things you HATE that bad networkers do at local events. On the right side, write down all the things you LOVE that great networkers do at local events.

Step 2:   Now think about how those behaviors manifest only.

Step 3:   Go do the things on the right.

Step 4:   Be patient.

Being a person of value who deserves trust takes time. But it will build quickly if you are sincere and helpful!

Pop Quiz

1. T/F: To have a successful podcast, you need at least 10,000 downloads a month. True fans.

2. T/F: Building rapport and trust takes time. But it's worth it.

3. T/F: "Always be pitching" is a motto for Facebook group engagement.

Answers:

1. F - "Success" from a podcast comes in so many different forms [remember our tree!]. Make sure you know what your goals are and what success looks like to you.

2. T - Keep adding value and interacting, and you will quickly grow the "know, like and trust" factor.

3. F - Constantly talking about what you are selling is off-putting. Act online like you would offline. Give, give, give, then ask.

2.12: Artful Emails

What is it?

UNLESS YOU LIVE UNDER a rock, you know what an email is!

But you may not realize just how many you end up sending directly related to maintaining and growing a successful podcast.

You find yourself emailing:

- Potential guests
- Confirmed guests
- Guests whose show just went live (asking them to share)
- Potential hosts to interview you
- Your email list to feature episodes and special guests
- Etc.

Why should podcasters care? Benefits to your brand and business

You only get one chance to make a great first impression. In fact, you have less time than you think.

30 seconds? 7 seconds? 3 seconds? 1/10th of a second?

According to a series of experiments by Janine Willis and Alexander Todorov out of Princeton University, all it takes is 1/10th of a second to form an impression of a stranger from their face.

And being exposed to the face longer does not significantly change those impressions, but they can reinforce your confidence in your gut reaction. [71]

This is for faces, sure.

There's great biological reasoning behind why we MUST be quick to judge and could pay dearly if we were wrong.

Imagine you are a caveman long before technology and grocery stores on each corner. Long before you could hope in a car or on a plane to explore near and far.

You are alone gathering nuts and firewood and suddenly out of nowhere a burly man appears. He's a stranger to you. You have never seen him before and he is not dressed like your clan.

---

[71] Source:
https://www.princeton.edu/main/news/archive/S15/62/69K40/index.xml?section=topstories

What does he want? Will he harm or help you? Does he need help or is he looking to steal your vital resources?

You have a split second to assess the situation and decide if you should fight, flee, or stay...

Under these circumstances for hundreds of thousands of years, we humans have genes that were selected by natural selection to favor those who could make quick and accurate judgments. (Those who couldn't often fell victim and were more likely to die off and not live long enough to reproduce).

This is why we are so attuned to reading facial expressions and body language. Even if you cannot explain why you have a bad feeling about someone, it is because of the unspoken cues you have picked up on.

For this very reason, I propose this is why we ladies tend to notice and analyze subtle cues and unspoken communication.

I know for me that there has been many a time that I have said to my male friends or husband, "Did you SEE the look she gave me when I said 'XYZ'?!?!" and they in turn look at me like I am crazy. "I didn't see see anything. You are reading into it." Am I???

Or because we are female and biologically weaker physically (on average) than 50% of the population, did we need to heighten those senses and ability to process non-verbal cues even faster and in-depth?

...okay...long story short...

Even if we are talking about business online, you have far less time to make a great first impression than you may have previously thought.

Then, confirmation bias kicks in.

Confirmation bias is our predisposition to look for information that reinforces our beliefs. Who can forget the 2016 election?

Ask any avid Donald Trump or Hillary Clinton supporter to look at a political situation and I bet you $10,000 that each picks out details from the story that reinforces their own beliefs, ignoring evidence to the contrary.

We all do this.

So, if you make a bad first impression (in the first few seconds!), we next just look for information to support our gut feeling that you aren't great.

This goes for in-person networking, website design, and... emails.

Emails!?

Yep.

Send me a long, stream of consciousness, disjointed email and I will make judgments about you like this:

- unprofessional

- disorganized

- discourteous

- unintelligent

Or I will just ignore it and not read it al all.

Fair or not, how you communicate also communicates about you and your business!

You are bleeding business and leaving a wake of business-relationship-destruction if you are haphazardly shooting off sloppy, disjointed emails.

And if you think that is too extreme, okay, you are certainly not impressing the bigger fish you want to impress and collaborate with. They ain't got no time for that. [Intentional grammar error.]

Laura's experience

I have become known for clear emails with lots of detail presented in a way that people can easily consume and act upon.

In part, this originated from being so frustrated by crazy, haphazard emails I would get in business. I felt aggravated and annoyed. I'd have to spend SO much time sorting through giant blobs of stream of consciousness to extract what I actually needed to know and the next action I needed to take.

So, I started to structure my own emails in the way that I wish I received them from others.

In Brandon T. Adam's first Influencer Mastermind Accelerator Program[72], he asked us each to email him our obstacles, goals, and what we want out of the mastermind.

The next time we talked, he said that the email I sent was the most thorough, thoughtful, and clear he received. He could tell I put a lot of effort into it and appreciated the way I communicated it all. I showed that I respected his time because it was easy for him to scan and mentally process. I showed that I was professional and committed because of the detail and organization.

This was my first written opportunity to make an impression with a big fish.

What impression is his mind now looking for evidence to reinforce?

Okay, so let's tie this into podcasting.

---

[72] http://livetogrind.com/influencer

Assuming you both want to conduct interviews and be interviewed by other podcasters (Pro Tip: The latter is one of the best ways to grow your own audience!), you will be communicating via email or via writing online.

I know that as a podcaster, I write the following emails often to:

- book guests
- inspire guests to share their episodes
- make introductions between guests
- thank guests for coming on the show
- pitch being interviewed on others' shows
- thank other hosts for interviewing me

10 best tips for effective emails [to get opens and replies]

1. Structure an email like you would a book (just way shorter).

a) Use headlines

b) Use bold to call out subsections

c) Use bullets instead of paragraphs when you have multiple ideas on the same topic

2. Don't use tons of fonts and colors.

a) The more visual variety you have, the more the reader has to 'figure out' what you are trying to communicate, if anything.

b) If you are going to highlight something in yellow or use red text, it better be for a really big main point. Don't overdo it or we'll just glaze over it.

3. Add 'negative space' between chunks so the entire thing does not look so ominous and blob-like.

4. Hyperlink things out you want the reader to have access to.
Do not force them to go search for it if you can provide the source directly for them.

5. When you are done writing, go back through it to proofread and ensure clarity.

   a) Read it aloud

   b) Check that the logical flow makes sense (rearrange or edit, if not)

6. If you are writing to more than one person, call out their name at the front, or just above, chunks relevant to them and bold their name so they can quickly jump to that area.

7. Try to address benefits of whatever you are writing about at the top of the email.
Remember, no one cares what you want. We care what we want.

8. Use parentheses or brackets to call out important details or side notes.

   a. For example, if I am describing images and PDFs, I will write [see attachment] or [image attached] to reinforce that there is another asset that goes along with what I am writing.

   b. This also helps me doublecheck I included all I meant to when I proofread. I see the brackets and check to make sure all is attached that I called out.

9. Begin and end with cordial salutations.

a) [intro example]
Hi, _____!
So great talking with you yesterday. Glad your trip to Paris was amazing!
To follow up on helping you get more opt-ins from your landing page....

b) [outro example]
Thanks again for your insights!
Hope you have a great weekend,
Laura

10. Insert your own personality into it, as appropriate.

a) Personally, I am a huge fan of smiley emojis. It helps soften how words sound and shows that I am happy to communicate with the person.

b) I also write in a playful manner because that is my style in real life. I can turn this up or down depending on the recipient and context, but each thing I write is uniquely in my voice. Or at least I like to think so. ;)

Okay, let's throw a bonus tip into the mix!

Bonus tip: Email templates

I hate...hate...hate. Did I mention hate? Redundancy.

Wasted efforts. Squandered time.

We have so little time to accomplish all we want in business!

So, if you are writing similar emails over and over, write one KILLER one once. Then save it as a template and just adjust it for the next person.

That's what I have done with all my podcast related emails.

Here's how:

1. In Gmail (or any email service), I'll write a killer email and send it off, BCCing myself.

2. Now I'll receive a copy of that email and I'll drop it into a Gmail folder with templates or just take mental note of the email subject line I used.

3. Next time I need to see that email, I'll:

   a. Search for the email subject line (or in the folder)

   b. Click "Forward"

   c. Take the "FWD:" out of the subject line

   d. Edit the few pieces in the email to make it personal to the new person

   e. Doublecheck that you didn't leave any inapplicable text in the email - proofread

   f. And send!

You can also copy and paste the whole email into a Google Doc and save it in a folder in Google Drive. Then you can copy and paste the email into a new message next time you need it, personalize it, and send it off.

Either way, you are saving yourself tons of time and mental bandwidth. Plus, you are ensuring each recipient is getting your best work.

Great examples

Email 1

Here's a copy of the email I send to podcast guest invitees. I have revised it over time as I have sent it off and now just customize the top and hit send.

It's long, but easy to scan.

4. Guest's best advice for someone just starting out ...and further along.

5. Most recommended tools / books / tactics, etc.

6. Freebie/promo giveaway we can link out on shownotes. (if you have something?) or discount code for listeners of the show on courses/products.

7. How can the audience learn more about you?
- Website, email, social media you are comfy sharing.

A GREAT TIP:
Think ahead on a catchy show title for your episode and think of ways to hit on that concept. For example:
- "3 Ways You're Doing Social Media Wrong and How to Fix It in 5 Minutes or Less"
- "The 5 Best Hacks for Better Sales Copywriting"
- "Important Lessons Learned from Failure-Turned-Around in Facebook Ad Copy & Design"
- "Psychology Hacks That Earn Your Business Money"

You do not have to title the episode, but if you think in this way for content to prepare talking points on, it will be more interesting for the listener and help me write a killer title to garner more listens.

BONUS: If time permits and you are comfortable, I will ask these after the official recording is done to use in future mash-up episodes or bonus materials (TBD):
1. Favorite inspirational quote and why?
2. If you had to start all over knowing what you know now, what is 1 thing you would do differently?
3. Most embarrassing business story? (if comfy)
4. What fear/block/challenge are you working on right now?
5. If you had a biz board of directors - living or deceased - what 5 people would you put on it?

The Fine Print
By scheduling an interview time and coming on the podcast, you, the guest, retain all copyrights to any content that you own and choose to share. By participating in the Copy That Pops podcast (CTP), you expressly authorize CTP to record, distribute, and disseminate materials produced in any manner as well as to utilize your likeness in advertising, marketing, or in any other manner as it so chooses. CTP or its respective assigns will hold all rights to the produced media of all types, as well as licensing, for future use in speeches, books, instructional materials, products, promotion, marketing, and in all other public distribution, and to charge for same, including, but not limited to, receipt of advertising or sponsorship fees. You waive all rights to receive payment of any kind for your participation in the recording.

Looking forward to talking more and shining some light on the great things you are working on!

Laura

PS: Attached are 9 Important Sound Tips for getting the best audio we can!
Note that a direct connection to the router is a must. Wifi is too shaky and degrades the quality the listeners hear

Laura Petersen, MAED
CopyThatPops.com

Let's connect! :)

Even the PDF of 9 Sound Tips for Hosts and Guests is already attached when I forward it on. [I'll add that to the Book Freebies[73] too]. And the guest gets tons of information so they feel at ease knowing what to expect in the interview.

Email 2

___

[73] http://www.podcastteachers.com/book-freebies/

Here's a copy of the email I send to podcast guests when their show is live. I just add in their relevant information (or have my assistant do it) and send it off to encourage them to share the episode.

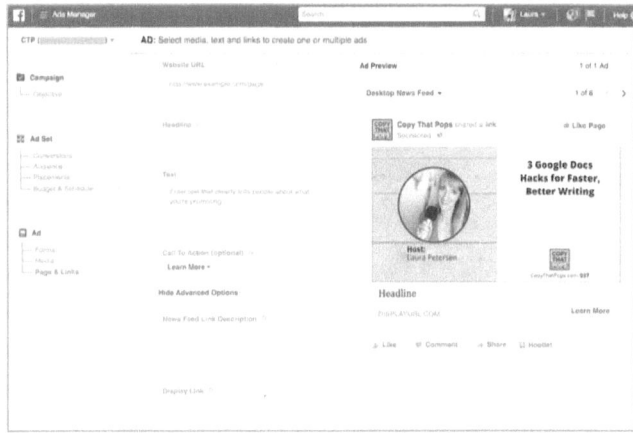

You'll notice that there are 4 images in the email as well. I create 4 custom images using the show title and quotes from the guest to promote on social media.

I give these to the guest too so they have something they can easily share as well. Plus it makes them feel honored that time and attention is taken to shine attention on their episode.

In the email, I try to stick to important elements and make it very clear how they can share. No long paragraphs that eat up their time to slog through.

Bullets and strategic bolding are everybody's friends.

Email 3

Here is an example email from our influencer in the next section, Marcus Meurer and his company DNX Global which caters to digital nomads who love to work from anywhere in the world.

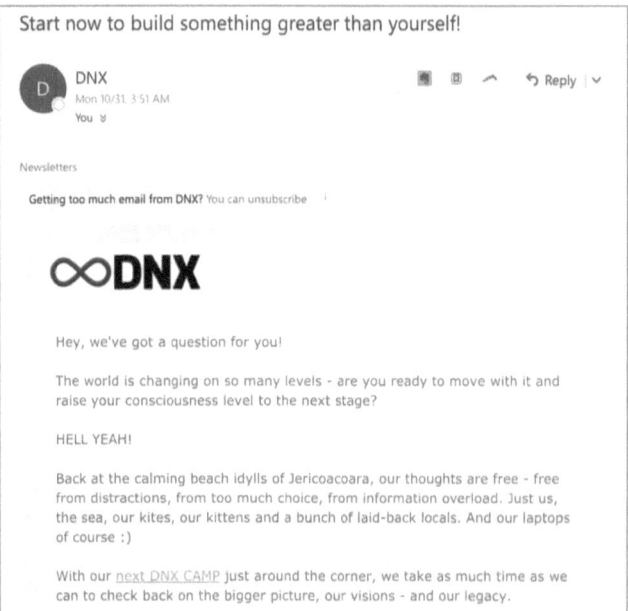

Remember when Marcus wrote about the Nomad Bubble? Wow, things have changed a lot since then! The priorities for many of our digital nomad friends really shifted. From "how can *I* achieve freedom and independence" towards "how can I serve *the world* and create an impact"... AWESOME!

Building on that, here's something we've been pondering on in the last days: The concept of different levels of consciousness. It's such an interesting topic, so we gotta share it with you...

The four levels of consciouscness are:
1. Egocentric
2. Ethnocentric
3. Worldcentric
4. Cosmocentric

Right now, about 70% of humanity is shifting from ego- to ethnocentric. It's not just about themselves anymore. People extend their awareness to a bigger tribe, a like-minded crowd they belong to. Realizing that if we want to evolve, we have to give and share.

BUT there's a small but growing number of people, who think a bit different. Who are not happy with how our world works. Money-driven capitalism is outdated, jobs security doesn't exist, our education system is outdated.

Instead, we want to consume less, eat more healthy food, be more spiritual, meditate, connect with locals and take care about life ourselves... Agree?

If so, that means you're likely to be part of the 5% or so who are world centric. That's true for many people in our community. Our identity isn't linked to just one place and we're open to care about people on a global level!

This is not where you want to stay though!

There's another stage: The cosmo centric mind has empathy for all beings in the world. Not just humans, but nature, animals, plants and our planet as a whole. It's the highest level of consciousness. And we believe *everyone* should try to achieve this...

We're super fascinated and grateful for all the things location-independent life has taught us so far. Like knowing, that each of us can do his part, shaping our world, while working towards our dreams...

Times have never been better!
ARE YOU READY?

DNX COMMUNITY ★ IT's NOT ABOUT US
...it's about *ALL* of us! We are changing the world and building a community of people who live life to their fullest potentials.

That's why we're so passionate about the DNX Community. It's *free* and open to anyone! Nearly 1,500 members - exchanging skills, ideas, experiences and their best tips and hackz to live and work free and from anywhere.

You're not part of it yet? Then Join our DNX COMMUNITY NOW!

P.S: It's much easier & more fun to grow together. You think what we do could also be helpful for some of your friends? Great!
Start sharing & invite your friends to join the movement!

DNX PODCAST ★ Latest Episodes

While traveling and working remotely, we meet lots of passionate digital nomads and successful entrepreneurs on the road...

Marcus gets them in front of the mic for you to extract their best tips & learnings on the DNX LIFE HACKZ podcast.

Check out the latest episodes with some participants from the DNX CAMP Lemnos and interviews with Eric the founder of Copass and Tijana a longterm Digital Nomad.

Listen, subscribe and pls leave a review on iTunes.

> **TUNE IN TO THE BEST EPISODES ON THE DNX PODCAST >>**

Stay in touch with us on Instagram, Snapchat, Facebook & Twitter

YOU HAVE EVERYTHING YOU NEED TO BUILD SOMETHING FAR GREATER THAN YOURSELF // Seth Godin

Lots of Love & Energy from Jericoacoara
Feli & Marcus

Lots of Love & Energy from Jericoacoara
Feli & Marcus

Feli's Bio ⅄ Marcus' Bio
Feli on Twitter ⅄ Marcus on Twitter
Feli on Facebook ⅄ Marcus on Facebook
Feli on Instagram ⅄ Marcus on Instagram
Feli on Medium ⅄ Marcus on Medium
Marcus on Snapchat

www.dnxhub.com
www.dnxglobal.com
www.dnxcamp.com

Facebook: www.facebook.com/dnx
Twitter: www.twitter.com/dnxglobal
Instagram: www.instagram.com/dnxglobal

nomads and successful entrepreneurs on the road...

Marcus gets them in front of the mic for you to extract their best tips & learnings on the DNX LIFE HACKZ podcast.

Check out the latest episodes with some participants from the DNX CAMP Lemnos and interviews with Eric the founder of Copass and Tijana a longterm Digital Nomad.

Listen, subscribe and pls leave a review on iTunes.

TUNE IN TO THE BEST EPISODES ON THE DNX PODCAST >>

Stay in touch with us on Instagram, Snapchat, Facebook & Twitter

YOU HAVE EVERYTHING YOU NEED TO BUILD SOMETHING FAR GREATER THAN YOURSELF // Seth Godin

Lots of Love & Energy from Jericoacoara
Feli & Marcus

INSIGHTS FROM AN INFLUENCER: MARCUS MEURER

Bio

Marcus is an entrepreneur and digital nomad who loves creating amazing projects and following his passion to live the life of his dreams, traveling around the world.

Originally from Germany, Marcus founded DNX GLOBAL[74] as the first conference for digital nomads on the topic of location-independent working and online independence.

The DNX movement[75] was kicked off with the German-speaking event DNX BERLIN[76] in May 2014.

From there, he organized the first DNX CAMP[77] in Tarifa, Spain and Lisbon, Portugal during the summer of 2015. He and his partner Felicia Hargarten have gone on to host many more in spots like Brazil, Greece [where I met Marcus], Thailand, and Mexico.

Camps include coworking, sports, and living healthy with a focus on inspirational talks from entrepreneurs, mastermind collaboration, goal setting, and mindfulness.

---

[74] http://www.dnxglobal.com/
[75] http://www.dnxhub.com/
[76] http://www.dnx-berlin.de/
[77] http://www.dnxcamp.com/

In addition to the DNX world, he offers a variety of services including:

- Online Angels[78]: advises businesses in online marketing, conducts analyses, develops traffic strategies, and helps with operative implementation.

- Rock My Site[79]: develops websites for companies and freelancers with modern designs. [German]

- Travelicia[80]: one of the biggest travel blogs on the topic of Backpacking and Adventure Travel. [German]

- Trendings[81]: a blog about trends and news in the world of tech. [German]

In addition to his own projects, Marcus is a startup investor in companies like Protonet[82], Userlike[83], Sugar Shape[84], Bloomy Days[85] and Blue Patent[86].

His podcast Life Hackz Show[87] (with episodes in both German and English) gets over 80,000 downloads a month and is #1 in iTunes (Germany) in the competitive Business category, even beating out Gimlet's StartUp Podcast.

---

[78] http://www.onlineangels.de/
[79] http://www.rockmysite.de/
[80] http://www.travelicia.de/
[81] http://www.trendings.de/
[82] http://www.protonet.info/
[83] http://www.userlike.com/
[84] http://www.sugarshape.de/
[85] http://www.bloomydays.com/
[86] http://www.bluepatent.com/
[87] http://www.lifehackz.co/new-here/

Insights from Marcus

Because I met Marcus at one of his DNX Camps in Lemnos, Greece in June of 2016 (which was absolutely amazing), I am also on his email list.

And I have been beyond impressed with the emails that he sends out to his 'tribe.' They are detailed, clear, compelling, and full of great information that inspires you. And you are able to apply the information right away.

They also are terrific at driving traffic back to his podcast and social media profiles.

So, I asked Marcus if he would answer a few questions on how he approaches his artfully crafted emails.

Below is the transcription of his insights that he sent to me via audio, which I will run as a podcast episode back at Copy That Pops.

You can also hear podcast episodes that we recorded with each other in-person in Greece here:

• My interview of Marcus Meurer:

http://copythatpops.com/016

• Marcus interviews me for the Life Hackz Show:

http://copythatpops.com/me-on-the-hot-seat

Now here are Marcus's amazing insights on effective emails!

———~~~———

Marcus:

So, thanks for your compliment on our emails.

It's a hell of a lot of work but it's also a hell of a lot of fun.

I'll go through your questions.

1. What makes a great email to your community?

So, what we are thinking about when we start to write our monthly newsletter is, "What is the highest value we can give to our community?"

So, what are they keen to know about?

What would they benefit from?

Always going from the egocentric to the cosmocentric to what could we give back to the people?

So what are the people looking for?

And going through our last emails, for instance, it's sharing our news or our best tools and hacks for starting into the digital nomad lifestyle.

We just started this huge resource list on dnxglobal.com/tools where we put weeks or even months of work into it and now give it away for free.

And this for sure goes then into our newsletter.

So, it's not just our newsletter, I think it begins even before that. We really, really care about our people.

We really care about our community.

We really care that everybody gets the most from our knowledge that we could give and be as free and authentic and open to anybody in this community.

So, for instance, in the last email I think it was like the tools list we just created, then we shared some podcast episodes which could be beneficial, which is also for free. Then we shared the best job offers on our DNX job board which are also all for free.

In the beginning, which is very important, which I also do in my podcast episodes, we always get a little bit personal because people are also interested in Feli [Marcus's girlfriend and Co-Founder Felicia] and me and where we are, what we are doing, what our plans are (in terms of travel plans but also business plans), our vision for the future, when the next camps will happen, and when the next events will happen.

And since this is so tightly close to our personal brands and to our personal stories, it doesn't seem too pushy and too salesy when we talk about our camps and conferences because this is our life. And this is how we sustain our travels and this is why we are traveling when we are traveling to different parts of the world. We are doing location scouting all over the world and setting up partnerships, corporation site events, pre-events, the main event, the workshop, the masterminds.... And this is all about what we are doing in our lives.

[Lots of wind blowing in the background!]

I hope you still can understand me because Jeri [Jericoacoara, Brazil] is a cool kite spot. There's lots of wind!

2. How to organize emails so they are clear and engaging.

We always optimize our draft and our framework of the newsletter. And we try lots of different stuff.

In MailChimp you can even send out A/B campaigns to test which gives you more attention and more interaction.

So, in the beginning we used lots graphic designs and put lots of work into it. And now we are more into this new elegant, plain style with just our logo.

I think this is also a good takeaway to be willing to adapt and to change. Especially what your people are looking for. I think what differentiates us from other businesses and products is that our design is always very clear and very professional. And very state of the art.

And so, I'm not afraid of changing anything in the design as long as it gives our identity and corporate design a shiny, cool, professional look. So, it's all about being professional but still approachable and personal.

This is what our brand DNX should communicate and this is why the logo is very plain and simple. But I think from a design perspective also really, really beautiful.

3. How do you encourage people to listen to the podcast and share with friends?

In the beginning I did a raffle, giving out DNX tickets for every review I got. And announcing the rules of the raffle, I also asked for subscriptions and shares with friends once in a while.

-- But I don't overuse it. --

Once in a while I'll ask people directly in the episode to share with their friends. To share it with their family. To share it even with their mom, with their dad, etc.

Listeners who write to me that they shared it with their family and now they're also listening to it. Sometimes I ask the listeners to share it with 3 people who could benefit from the content.

[Sounds of dishes clanking from the camp.]

And I encourage people to listen to the podcast. We also post outstanding episodes in our DNX community.

For instance, now I decided to publish the DNX Talks for free on the DNX podcast. So every Tuesday, an episode goes out of a whole DNX talk. People love it, they rave about it, and I post it in the community.

It's all about giving, giving, giving. Like 10 times giving. And one time asking for something and then people will, yeah, they will "run your house." They're just waiting for you to ask for something and then they will do whatever you want.

And I think this is a very good strategy. At least it works for us to give like 10 times more than you take or ask.

So the ratio from what we give out for free and what we ask money for is like 10 to 1.

4. How do you give your audience lots of value in your emails that they can easily apply?

In addition to the podcast episodes I always do show notes. And I also give short descriptions explaining it a little bit further (what I was talking about) and giving them some backlinks and how people can execute and apply what they hear.

We always try to get them committed like you've seen on our camps. We have this goal check-ins, and the business check-ins, present goals. In our emails, we ask feedback.

In the email cycle, we ask people what is your biggest obstacle? What is your challenge at the moment?

And they start to reply and we go into discussions with them.

We engage with them a lot in our DNX community. I'm there everyday. Feli's there everyday. And we help where we can.

And I think this is also a secret which makes us very personal, approachable and close and linked to our peeps. To our tribe. And this helps them also to apply and execute.

Wonderful advice from Marcus! He and Feli really have built an amazing community of digital nomads around their company DNX Global. I actually look forward to their emails, so that tells you something about the quality and value that they give.

Follow their lead with your own emails!

How to implement this right now

Step 1: Make a list of 5 emails you send over and over again.

Step 2: Pick 1 of them and write the best version of it that you ever have.

Step 3: Save this email in your email or in a file for future use.

Step 4: Next time you need to send this email, copy and paste it in, personalize it, and send!

Step 5: Repeat this process until you have no more redundancy and crystal-clear emails for your podcast.

[You can then start having a virtual assistant (V.A.) process some of these on your behalf and save yourself even more time.]

Pop Quiz

1. How long do we have to make a great first impression, approximately?

   _____

2. What are your emails currently communicating about you, your podcast, and your business? (Be honest! :))

   _____

   _____

3. What benefits could you received by improving your email communication? Name 3 or more.

   _____

   _____

   _____

Answers:

No answer key from me on this one!

Instead, share your thoughts with me:

Snap me @LaptopLaura on Snapchat

Tweet me @LapropLaura on Twitter with the hashtag #CopyBook. I want to hear from YOU!

2.13: Booking More Podcast Interviews with a 1-Sheeter

What is it?

LET'S SAY YOU WANT a job (I know, I know...perish the thought, right entrepreneurs? Stick with me a minute. I do have a point.)

And you even know someone who knows someone who's hiring for your dream position.

What is the most likely next step you would take?

A. Show up at the office and demand an interview.

B. Send the hiring manager all your high school and college transcripts, along with that 100-page memoir you're working on.

C. Email a professional note (making sure to make benefits to the hiring manager clear) with your resume attached.

D. None of the above. It's too self-promote-y to reach out to the hiring manager.

If you answered C, you are correct!

Now, there are more creative ways to garner attention of people making decisions, but a pithy, professional email with a stellar-looking resume is a great first start.

So, let's take this scenario to the podcasting world.

Other podcasters are the "hiring managers" and your 1-sheeter PDF is the "resume."

Why should podcasters care? Benefits to your brand and business

As of 2016, about 55% of Americans know what the term "podcast" means. [According to Edison research[88].]

So anytime you share the news about your podcast with the world, about half of people listening do not even know what a podcast is.

This recently happened to me when I went out to dinner with my aunt. I tried to explain that a podcast is like a radio show that anyone can create, anyone can listen to for free, and anyone can play it anytime.

It took a while to convey it because she had no idea about podcasts at all.

Once I downloaded my show and a few others in her field, it clicked and she was excited to listen.

But think about your efforts here. If you tell 100 random people in your network, only 55 will know what a podcast is. And still less may know how to even get a podcast to play, even though they know the term. Assuming a 25% conversion rate of "sure, I'll take a listen," that is about 14 potential new listeners.

GROUP 1

1000 people = sample size

550 know what a podcast is

138 decide to listen (25% conversion rate)

---

[88] http://www.edisonresearch.com/wp-content/uploads/2016/05/The-Podcast-Consumer-2016.pdf

What if, instead however, we could tell 100 people who ALREADY knew what a podcast was AND how to play it?

GROUP 2

1000 people = sample size

1000 know what a podcast is

250 decide to listen (25% conversion rate)

That's nearly twice as many people.

In this example, that's an extra 190 new listeners. But imagine if the sample sizes were bigger! Growth potential is far better in group 2.

But how do I get in front of people from group 2?

Easy.

Be interviewed on other podcast shows.

Write this down:

One of the best, most effective ways to grow your own podcast is to be interviewed on other podcasts.

Back to our analogy with the resume.

Once you are ready to extend past your network to book interviews, you are going to be reaching out to people who do not know you and likely do not have time or interest to listen to your show in-depth before deciding to have you on. At least not at the outset.

Just like a hiring manager first filters through applicants by looking only at their resume and "cover letter" or accompanying email, so too does a podcast host and his or her team need to shift through loads of inquiries to find the gems and invite them on.

If you want to be a gem plucked from the crowd, you need to stand out. You need to look professional. You need to make things easy on them.

Laura's experience

I was put in contact with a company just a few weeks into my podcast who said they had some clients who would be wonderful guests on my show. How wonderful!

I was new to it and happy to make more great connections.

The gentleman from Interview Connections[89] (founded by Jessica Rhodes) then sent me an easy to read and easy to scan email with 1 sentence highlights of 5 guest opportunities for me. Then, attached, were 1-sheeter PDFs for each of them with their photo, some biographical information, claims to fame, social media profiles, and even "great questions to ask me!" bulleted out.

Wow. They just made my life so much easier as a host!

They took the researching out of it. I could instantly see the person from the photo and identify indicators of success and professionalism with awards listed out, a quality headshot, and nicely designed layout.

As I have grown my show and more people are reaching out to me with requests to be interviewed, I now look out for pitches that have

---

[89] http://www.interviewconnections.com/

MY interests in mind. Make it simple for ME. Help me make BOTH of us look good.

A 1-sheeter, therefore, is a must!

But no stress. You don't need to spend a ton on a great one. I'll give you some tools and tips in the "How to implement this right now" section.

Great examples

Here are a few of those first ones I received.

This one from Lee Caraher has a bit too much text for my personal taste, but what is written is really interesting! And you see she is an author and a game creator with just a quick glance!

You can also quickly see all her social media and contact information (I blocked out a few lines with grey bars), saving the podcast host from having to go search it out! And Lee did not disappoint!

She was one of my favorite guests and we had never spoken until the interview. Listen at Copy That Pops[90].

I was very glad that Interview Connections[91] reached out to me to introduce her and made my saying "yes" so easy.

---

[90] http://copythatpops.com/014-2
[91] http://www.interviewconnections.com/

Same goes for this next example from our influencer in this chapter, Stephen Christopher.

I love how he's included two photos. One is "in action" showing that he is experienced on the microphone and a podcaster himself.

This 1-sheeter makes it easy as pie to want to book him and have all the information you'd need in one spot.

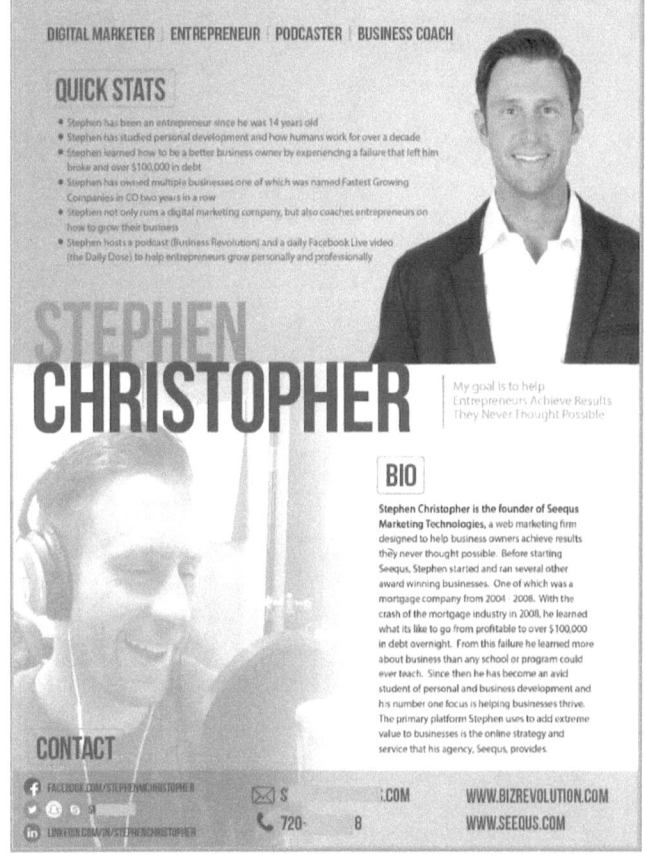

Lastly, here is mine!

It will go through some more edits as I test and see what works, but I wanted to show you my approach. I made it in Canva[92].

LauraPetersen

Entrepreneur · Teacher · Podcaster · Author · Speaker · Connector

Education

B.A. Psychology - UCLA
minor in German, honors

M.A.E.D. Education - UOP
with honors

- TEFL Certification
- Courses on Photoshop, Illustrator, InDesign
- Rescue Diver - Scuba

Topics

- Copywriting
- Psychology
- Podcasting
- Self-publishing #1 book

Fun Facts

- Flew in Zero G
- Tried out for Survivor 13x
- Traveled to 40+ countries
- Lived in Europe twice
- Lived with host families in Mexico & Costa Rica
- Vegan as of Jan. 2016
- Love Salsa dancing

Q&A

1. Why is copy important for podcasters?

2. What is a benefit of podcasting you didn't expect?

3. What are 3 keys to hitting #1 Amazon Best-Seller?

4. Tips for writing your first book? (in 30 days)

5. Is podcasting too saturated?

6. What do you believe about "failure"?

7. How can psychology help us in business?

Biz

Accelerant Media Group
Branding, PR, Crowdfunding
Co-Founded with Brandon T. Adams

Copy That Pops
Podcast:
CopyThatPops.com/podcast
Book: *Copywriting for Podcasters: How to Grow Your Podcast, Brand, and Business with Compelling Copy* (Hit #1)
CopyThatPops.com/book

Course: Become an Amazon Best-Selling Author with No Email List, Ad Budget, or Experience
CopyThatPops.com/abs

Contact

[f] [t] [o] [△] @LaptopLaura
[in] /in/LauraPetersen
[○] Laura.Petersen89
[✉] Laura@CopyThatPops.com

Bio, features, & photos to help with shownotes:
CopyThatPops.com/media

---

[92] http://canva.com/

INSIGHTS FROM AN INFLUENCER: JESSICA RHODES

Bio

Jessica Rhodes is the founder and CEO of InterviewConnections.com, the premier Guest Booking agency for podcasters and guest experts, and she is the acclaimed author of *#RockThePodcast From Both Sides of the Mic!*

Jessica is the host of Interview Connections TV, where each week she helps her viewers rock the podcast from both sides of the mic. She hosts/co-hosts three podcasts:

- Rhodes to Success[93]
- The Podcast Producers[94]
- The Parenting Rhodes[95]

The Podcast Producers was selected by Apple as a "How to Podcast" show in iTunes and has also been included in the syllabus for a course about podcasting and audio journalism at Western University in Ontario, Canada.

---

[93] http://www.jessicarhodes.biz/category/rhodes-to-success-podcast/

[94] https://itunes.apple.com/us/podcast/the-podcast-producers/id980287762?mt=2

[95] https://itunes.apple.com/us/podcast/parenting-rhodes-jess-jamie/id1131033556?mt=2

Jessica has been featured in Entrepreneur magazine and has been a speaker at Podcast Movement, Podfest.us, and Dream Business Academy. She lives in Rhode Island with her husband and two kids.

Advice directly from Jessica

Getting interviewed on podcasts as a guest expert is the best way to promote your podcast because you're being exposed to people who already subscribe to and listen to podcasts - talk about an easy sell!

My number one tip to guest experts is to have and use a 1-sheet when you get pitched to podcasters.

Imagine going to the grocery store to buy a box of cereal.

Instead of the colorful, descriptive boxes lining the shelves, all you find are plain brown boxes with price tags and a little note saying, "This box of cereal is perfect for you!"

It would be pretty hard to figure out which box was actually the one you wanted, right?

The same is true when you are pitching yourself as a guest expert without a 1-sheet.

How is a host supposed to say YES without getting a good picture of who you are?

A 1-sheet does just that.

It's a 1-page document that gives podcasters the exact information they need to know to decide if you are a good fit for their podcast and be prepared for an interview with you.

Your 1-sheet should have your bio written in third person, interview topics and questions, as well as your contact information including your websites and Skype name.

Lastly, don't skimp and send the hosts this information in a boring Word doc.

Work with a graphic designer or contact my team at Interview Connections so your 1-sheet is professionally designed and positions you as an in-demand expert!

Jessica lives and breathes podcasting and booking interviews, so take her sage advice to heart!

INSIGHTS FROM AN INFLUENCER: STEPHEN CHRISTOPHER

Stephen is back to share more insights.

To remind you from Chapter 2.7, he runs Seequs Digital Marketing[96] and the Business Revolution[97] pod-cast.

Direct Advice Quoted from Stephen

My best advice is to remember that business and life is supposed to be fun! Through all the ups and downs, it's a learning experience, without the valleys we could never experience the awesomeness of the mountain tops.

Now, here's some of his advice about a 1-sheeter.

[This below will also be featured as a podcast audio episode back at CopyThatPops.com/048.]

A 1-sheeter is your first opportunity to make an impression. There's so many podcasts out there now. There's a lot of people that want to be on your show so you have a very short amount of time to get somebody's attention, so a 1-sheeter is extremely important now.

It's just like websites. 5 or 6 years ago or maybe 7 years ago, websites had a lot of information on them and now we've had to cut down how much

---

[96] https://www.seequs.com/
[97] http://bizrevolution.com/

information we put on there because everybody's attention span is different.

1-sheeters now need to be very short, very concise, very to the point.

One of the things that I've taken into consideration, we have 3 primary modalities, meaning the ways that we learn and the different ways that people primarily interact.

We have auditory, kinesthetic, and visual.

One of the things that I started to do with my 1-sheeter is try to hit on all of those as much as I possibly can.

You want to have some sort of a visual. You want to have people get to know you a little bit. Have them feel good about you. That also goes over into kinesthetic a little bit.

Then the auditory piece, what does your actual text say?

One of the things I'm doing on my new 1-sheeter is I'm going to have a little intro video to myself so that people that really want to see who I am or how I communicate and what my tone is like and how fast I talk or how slow I talk or if people think I'm smart or whatever it is, people want to see who they're going to interact with.

I'm going to try get that out of the way so that people are more likely to book me by doing a short introduction video of just who I am, very casual, something like this.

Then I'll put a link to that on my 1-sheeter.

Now, the 1-sheeter should really be a place where somebody can go to get as much information as they want or need to in order to make a decision whether or not to have you on the show, really without ever having to go anywhere else.

I see a lot of 1-sheeters that come in for people asking to be on Business Revolution, where I really can't tell what they're going to talk about. I really can't tell who they are as a person.

I'm fortunate that I have Danielle [his assistant] to go out and listen to some of their podcasts and stuff like that and figure out if she thinks that they'd be a good fit for the show or sometimes I'll have to do a little interview with them just to see if they even are going to be a good guest for my audience and see if we're going to be a good fit when we're talking.

The 1-sheeter really is kind of a first impression and like I said, make sure that we're talking to all of the primary modalities of people: auditory, visual, kinesthetic.

The video is something that I'm going to try. I did that with an interview that we just did to hire new people for my digital marketing company. It went extremely well so I think that that's going to work out really well to have a little video link, "Meet Steven," or something like that.

I'll keep you posted on that but I think it's going to work well and I would definitely recommend it.

A lot of times people don't put a lot of work into their 1-sheeter. They rush through it, they just type up a bunch of stuff and it's so much easier to write a long 1-sheeter or a long letter or a long email than it is to really think about what you're trying to write and cut it down to as short amount of text as possible.

Put in time and energy into your 1-sheet.

This might be the only opportunity that you get to interview on somebody's podcast. If they don't like your 1-sheeter, even if you would be a great fit for somebody's show, they're never going to talk to you. They're never going to go out and listen to a podcast with you. Then when you pitch them again and again, they're going to just be like, "Nah. Sorry. I just didn't like you. I didn't like your 1-sheeter."

This is a true first impression so take time to figure out what you really want to put in your 1-sheeter. I guess a better way to say it would be take time to figure out what you don't want to put in your 1-sheeter and make sure it's very clear and very concise and very specific.

In marketing, I talk a lot about, "Don't try to be everything to everyone." Know what your subject matters are that you're fantastic at talking about and don't worry about the rest of the stuff.

Don't worry about getting it booked on tons and tons of shows.

Worry about getting booked on shows where your greatness is going to be able to shine. Invest some time in your 1-sheeter and try to make it honestly, as short as humanly possible. Make it very specific to what you're great at.

The last thing about the 1-sheeters that I have is remember, technically yes, the 1-sheeter is about you and what value you can add but think about it from a marketing standpoint. But you want to make sure that you're talking about what problems can you solve for them.

What value can you add to their audience?

What value can you add to their podcast?

Make sure that you're not making this 1-sheeter all about them. Make it about the problems you're going to solve. The content that you're going to give. The greatness that you're going to bring.

How you are going to help them to grow their show and that's going to make you much more likable on 1 sheet of paper. I think this is obvious, but make sure you have a picture or 2 of yourself. I would lean towards a real picture of you, not some fancy dolled-up picture of you or whatever.

I think the business headshot is kind of dying. I know that my last 1-sheeter had something like that but I'm moving away from that completely. It doesn't really tell a lot about you.

―――

I couldn't agree more with Stephen's input here!

Take a couple hours to make a great 1-sheeter and it will more than pay off in extra podcast gigs booked. It will also give you clarity in what you can talk about and help you feel less nervous as you get more interviews under your belt.

How to implement this right now

Step 1: Have a resume? Pull it out. Then set a timer for 5-7 minutes.

Step 2: On paper or digitally, add in bullets for:

- things you have done
- awards you have received
- classes you have taken
- certifications you have earned
- notable clients you've worked with
- events you have spoken at
- books you have written
- etc.

Pro Tip:

People love numbers. Numbers help us take things from general to specific.

So as you write what you have done, think about stats that can demonstrate your expertise.

E.g. "Grew email subscribers from 0 to 1,000 in 2.5 months."

E.g. "Sold $110,000 during new course launch."

E.g. "Been interviewed on over 250 podcasts!"

Step 3: Circle the items that are both impressive and relevant to the audiences of the hosts you will be seeking out. Or find ways to rephrase items that do not fit perfectly, but are still noteworthy.

Step 4: Decide what categories you will feature on your 1-sheeter. For mine, I have Education, Business, Q & A, Topics, Fun Facts, and Contact. But there is no one way to do it!

I'm a fan of bullets and breaking up text, so I tried to have a series of lists.

Pro Tip:

DO NOT have a bunch of big blobs of text.

Remember, ain't nobody got time for that. Make it EASY on the person deciding to talk to you or not.

Step 5: Time to create your 1-sheeter!

Handy with design?

Check out Canva. They have some templates that are a great place to start. Then you can adjust colors, words, and layout as desired.

Horrible with design?

Head over to Fiverr, UpWork, or 99Designs and pay someone to bring your vision to life.

Just make sure you have clarity in what you'd love to have as a final version so you can communicate it to them.

Step 6: Once you have your 1-sheeter, it's time to craft a short email with BENEFITS TO THE PODCAST HOST clearly addressed at the top. With your PDF attached for their review.

Step 7: Send off that email and the 1-sheeter to get those bookings! You can even share your 1-sheeter on LinkedIn, on your website (maybe under a "Media Inquiries" tab), or heck, even Instagram! Just make sure to blur out or remove contact information you do not want spread all over the web.

Step 8: Rock the interviews and watch your numbers skyrocket!

Pop Quiz

1. T/F: Squeeze as much text at possible onto your 1-sheeter, so you really impress the host.

2. What percentage of people (as of 2016) are familiar with the term "podcasting"?

    A. 47%

    B. 50%

    C. 55%

    D. 92%

3. Why is being interviewed on other podcasts such a great way to grow your own podcast?

    _____

    _____

    _____

    _____

Answers:

1. F

2. C

3. You can tap into the segment of the population who already knows what podcasting is and how to listen. Plus, they have an interest in doing so!

2.14: [BONUS] How to Book Guests Even When You Are Just Starting Out (High-Profile Ones Too!)

How I met this Influencer

IN OCTOBER OF 2016, I decided to join Brandon T. Adams's Mastermind Accelerator Program[98].

Inside his mastermind, I met about 20 other amazing entrepreneurs, many of whom have or are just starting podcasts.

One person in particular stood out.

Who is this guy and how is he booking such HUGE names on his podcast and it's not even launched yet?

Guests like...

- a millionaire by 17, 8 figures by 23
- a top growth hacker with 6 figures in monthly revenue

---

[98] http://bit.ly/BTA-accelerator

- an app developer with more than 2 million downloads and a new startup with platinum artists on board
- an award-winning Chef

Bernard Benjie Paraiso and I got to meet up in-person at the Thrive conference in San Diego at the end of October and he was kind enough to share with us all his amazing recipe for success.

We will get to it!

But first, a bit of biography background.

Bernard's Bio

Bernard Benjie Paraiso is an entrepreneur, digital marketing expert, and the host of "Views From 3B," a show where he shares insights from First

Class Entrepreneurs, Artists, and Philanthropists.

Learn more about him and mission at bernardbenjie.com and viewsfrom3b.com.

He's also used the techniques described below to connect and have awesome off the record conversations with big names like: Frank Kern, Nick Loper, Brandon T. Adams, John Lee Dumas, Tai Lopez, Joel Brown, and Tucker Max.

I'm sure they'll turn into podcast interviews soon enough!

Let's learn from Bernard...

INSIGHTS FROM AN INFLUENCER: BERNARD PARAISO

How to get your first guests when you start podcasting [and high-profile ones too!]

Advice straight from Bernard:

Congratulations! You just booked your event at the world's hottest venue! And now you need others to share the stage.

But wait, the tickets aren't sold yet and to the other artists, you're a no-name newbie.

So how do you get them to share to stage with you? How do you attract ticket-buyers?

In your case, the world's hottest venue is the internet.

The event is your podcast.

The crowd is your audience.

And the performers who share the stage are your podcast guests.

But how do you get guests to the share the stage without a huge raving audience or the household name to headline alongside you?

Answer:

In the words of Gary Vaynerchuk, "jab, jab, jab, right hook" or in non-VaynerNation talk: give, give, give, then ask.

Be A Giver

The best gifts we ever receive are always the ones that were specifically given with us in mind. The same goes for the most valuable thing we all have - time. For a high-level guest to be willing to share their time with you must first think, "what would be the biggest gifts for them?"

However, before we give our gifts it's important to keep in mind that all perceptions of gift givers aren't created equal.

Compare:

- A caramel candy offered to you by Grandma during Sunday dinner

vs.

- The same candy offered by a strange man with a beard driving by in his van

Don't be the strange man in the van!

Everyone is more open to receiving gifts from friends, family, and loved ones.

So, Step 1 is to be friendly and be a friend first.

Friends share common interests, values, goals, aspirations, connections, entertainment, and more.

So, the energy you must approach potential guests with shouldn't be one of a fanatic fanboy or fangirl, or worse - the plunderer who's coming to take their knowledge, their audience, and their resources with nothing in return.

It should be that of a friend who's traveling in the same direction.

Yes, that person may be more successful in some respects but that unique blend of experiences, upbringing, values, and DNA that makes you uniquely you, has only occurred once in the history of existence and never will again.

You're just as important and worthy of being heard, so treat potential guests like friends instead of Greek Gods on pedestals.

Keys to Giving

1. Do your research.

If possible, before you initially interact find out what they're currently working on, launching, or passionate about.

2. Be present.

Ask questions and prove that you were listening and that you care.

3. Drop pebbles in the same pond.

Social proof can go a long way in making potential connections more receptive and open to interactions with you. Be active in the same communities as your ideal guests and you'll be more likely to meet them or a mutual connection.

4. Be friendly.

In Jeffrey Gitomer's classic, "*Little Black Book of Connections*" he opens with, "All things being equal, people want to do business with their friends. All things being not quite so equal, people STILL want to do business with their friends."

5. Be confident.

You have plenty of good things to share and offer.

6. Be memorable.

Online - have a clear and concise vision for what you stand for and what you're looking to accomplish.

In-Person - stand out visually with something stylish, something technical, or through a friendly gesture like a well timed smile and greeting.

7. Be generous.

Adopt Gary Vaynerchuk's 51/49 philosophy and always strive to give more than you receive.

Ways to Give

1. The James Altucher Idea Machine Method

"Write a List of 10 Ideas That Can Help Them"

I recently saw James Altucher speak live at a recent conference and during his keynote he told the story of how he was able to connect with and interview the head of hospitality of AirBnB.

Being an unofficial expert from his travels and essentially living in AirBnB's for the past year, James had observed many things that he believed would improve the AirBnB guest experience and ultimately their impact and bottom line.

He listed them in a document, stored it, and continued on with his life. Months later during his travels, a mutual connection arose with someone at AirBnB and it turned out to be the head of hospitality whom James would later interview and work with.

2. Help Them "Find an apartment in a new city"

Esther Kiss, PR Expert and founder of "Born To Influence," coined the phrase during one of her talks where she described approaching offering value like helping an old friend find a new apartment in a new city.

If they're speaking in a city you're familiar with, recommend a list of awesome restaurants or great landmarks off the beaten path.

If they're looking to promote their new book through speaking, connect them with potential events you may be involved with.

If they're looking for reviews for their new course, order it and give it a try and leave an honest review.

If they're vegan, share awesome recipes, etc.

3. Build A Bridge

Trust their product or service? Recommend it to potential client. They're looking to make a certain type of connection? Make a quick one line intro for them via email or Facebook and CC them as well the potential client.

4. Offer Your Expertise Outside of Audience Exposure

When you're first starting out you may not have the 100k download counts or social media followers. However, you may be able to offer services a courtesy.

Writer? Write a blog post catering to their audience and send it to the potential guest for their review.

Photographer? Get photos of them on stage at an event and give it to them for free for their promotions.

Consultant? Give them a free introductory session.

The possibilities are endless.

Finding Guests

Now that you know how to build connections with potential guests, where do you find them?

Step 1: First, think through the traits of who your ideal guest is i.e. industry, expertise, personality, and etc. You need to know with whom you are looking to connect.

Step 2: Reach out to your current network and past guests and make the interview process as easy as possible. [Make it sound easy too.]

Instead of: "You're friends with XYZ right? Can you schedule coffee?"

Go for: "Thank you so much! If you have any friends or peers you think would be great guests for the show, a simple one line intro with them CC'ed in the message would be amazing and I could totally take care of the rest."

Pro Tip:

Instead of going back and forth on interview times via email, create an interview booking schedule with online tools such as:

- www.Calendly.com
- www.Acuityscheduling.com
- www.ScheduleOnce.com

Step 3: Identify where they interact and engage with others:

On marketplaces such as Amazon, check out the "new releases" section under books for authors in your industry or niche of choice.

Check out industry conference websites to identify upcoming and past speakers.

Attend conferences in person to connect with others in the industry as well as the organizers and speakers.

Join forums and Facebook groups where podcasters hang out and interact, engage, and build value within them. Your potential guests may be in there or someone connected to your ideal guests may be in there.

Guests of similar podcasts may be good people to reach out to as well. Often, in the shownotes of podcasts, there are ways to learn more about the guest and the ways to connect. You'd be surprised how reachable many big names are especially on emerging mediums such as Snapchat and Facebook Live.

Conclusion

In a nutshell, the key to booking potential guests is to shift your mindset to what you can get from them to what you can give to them and, ultimately, in the process you'll become a friend and person of value to your guests.

Then make it easy for everyone, and watch your podcast, brand, and business grow!

———

Wow, way to go Bernard for giving us SUCH incredible value to me for this book!

It was so good that I needed to give it its own bonus section.

Keep your eye on this influencer, folks!

Want More?

Still not convinced you can book great interview guests when you are new?

Let me share one last piece of advice from Adrian Aguilar's experience. He shared some great results on Facebook (we also met in Brandon's Influencer Mastermind Accelerator[99]) and I immediately asked him if he would share more details on it for you to benefit!

Quick Bio

Adrian Aguilar helps millennials find meaningful work and be successful in their careers or through entrepreneurism.

He jumped straight into entrepreneurship and podcasting when he quit his full-time job in June of 2016 [and wrote a massively viral blog about it on LinkedIn].

He is a Career Coach who focuses on personal development and hosts a podcast called Letsplore with the purpose of helping millennials figure out what they want to do with their lives.

---

[99] http://livetogrind.com/influencer

INSIGHTS FROM AN INFLUENCER: ADRIAN AGUILAR

When I first started podcasting, one of the biggest struggles I had was finding guests. Aside from tapping into family and friends, I was nervous no one else would want to come on my show. I quickly realized there are free services that help with this.

The services I found include:

- Interview Guests Directory[100]
- Help A Reporter Out[101]
- Radio Guest List[102]
- Source Bottle[103]

After submitting my info to Interview Guests Directory, Radio Guest List, and Source Bottle, I was quickly approved. Within 24 hours, I had over 100 requests of people who wanted to be on my show!

Help A Reporter Out took a little longer to get approved. Once I did, I received over 40 requests within three hours.

The problem now is not finding guests but screening guests to determine who the best fit is. I quickly realized there will never be a shortage of people wanting to be interviewed on podcasts, you just have to look in the right areas.

---

[100] www.interviewguestsdirectory.com/
[101] www.helpareporter.com/
[102] www.radioguestlist.com/
[103] www.sourcebottle.com/

This should come as a relief to new podcasters. Do not let "I do not know who I will interview" be an obstacle for you to get started.

2.15: [BONUS] How to Write Facebook Ad Copy to Promote Your Podcast Like a Pro

How I met this Influencer

I HAD BEEN A long-time fan of Josh and Jill from Screw the Nine to Five (and remember that you heard insights from Jill back in Chapter 2.9).

Not only are their web copy and lead magnet games on point, but so are their email sequences.

Each email I got from them made me want to take the action they had planned.

And through each email I felt like I knew them.

That's great copy.

So, then out of the blue appears Amanda Bond, The Ad Strategist.

I got an email from Jill about Facebook ads (automated with Infusionsoft, I'm sure of it) and clicked a link or replied back. And a few days later I got an email from Amanda.

And when I scrolled down in the thread, I saw Jill had forwarded it to Amanda saying something like, "Laura is interested! Cool, we'd love to have her on board."

I was like....wait a minute. What is this sorcery?

I knew they had most of this automated, but it looked so personalized! They were up to something smart and effective with their emails.

So, I responded to Amanda, saying that I loved what they were doing with emails. Super slick.

She responded with something like, "If you like our emails, imagine how we can help with your Facebook ads."

That led to a back and forth email conversation between the two of us and my checking out more of her stuff.

A month or so later, Screw the Nine to Five and Bond teamed up to launch ADdicted, a Facebook ads course.

I signed up, sprung for the Bootcamp VIP package to get more direct access to Bond and Josh, and learned a ton.

Since then, I've stayed in touch and always learn from their digital copy and quality content.

When Bond said, "yes!" to contribute some valuable insights to this book, I jumped at it.

Amanda Bond, The Ad Strategist

Over the years, she's learned from personal experience and the school of hard knocks about what works and what doesn't. And what CONVERTS—like gangbusters.

Instead of soapboxing vague methodologies to the entrepreneurial masses, she's down and dirty in the trenches with some seriously elite clients. So, if you want a step-by-step, cutting-edge strategy ripped straight from real experience, she's your go-to.

It's time to learn the RIGHT WAY to do Facebook Ads. Stop guessing. Start getting results.

INSIGHTS FROM AN INFLUENCER: AMANDA BOND

Bond and I jumped on a Skype call a few days before this book launched to squeeze in this amazing extra bonus for you!

The transcript below is from our conversation. You can also find the audio version of our talk back at CopyThatPops.com/podcast.

———

Bond:

So, tell me what you're working on, what you're doing.

Laura:

A book. The book is on *Copywriting for Podcasters*. It's all about how to grow the podcast, brand, and business with writing, because I think a lot of people go into podcasting thinking, "Oh, I suck at writing. I'll just do this."

But when the bots and the search engines and people come visit you, the first thing they see are the words or that's the only way that they can get that first impression.

Same with ads too, no one is going to jump from an ad to your podcast if it's not compelling somehow with the words and the creative image too.

Bond:

I love that.

Laura:

I thought if you could talk about ad copy in general and/or if you've got some with that client you're working on now specifically around podcasters, awesome.

Bond:

Yeah, for sure.... Maybe how to overcome the key challenges that we have with Facebook ads?

Laura:

Yeah, for sure.

Bond:

Like the major challenges, the fact that you're sending somebody to a page that you can't pixel. You can't track that entire customer journey, so you need to be extra compelling in your copy because if not, you're going to lose them along the way.

Laura:

Yeah, that's great.

Bond:

Does that make sense?

Laura:

Yeah. You mean like to iTunes. You can't pixel iTunes.

Bond:

You can't pixel iTunes, you can't pixel SoundCloud unless they're on the page that you're doing it and then you don't know if that particular view was attributed to the Facebook ad itself. It's just being very persuasive and giving them a damn good reason to get over there in general.

Laura:

What would you say, in general, to anyone who was trying to have an effective Facebook ad around the copy?

Bond:

For podcasts. I would say that it's really about connecting with why somebody would want to take the time to listen, right?

Podcasts are a commitment.

They're a freaking awesome commitment because a lot of the people that I follow in this space that I've found have been through podcasts, but it's not just simply giving an email address and receiving a download. It's actually a commitment.

To get people interested in taking that commitment with you, it's got to really speak to them.

It's got to speak to either a pain point or a desire that they have and not just be about, "Hey, here's my new podcast. Click on over and check it out."

At that point with the copy, you need to make it really, truly about your audience along the way.

Laura:

Can you give an example of one that maybe you've been seeing or worked on recently that was so compelling with what they wrote that people really were like, "Okay, I have to listen to this episode."

Bond:

Yeah, I have a client right now whose brand is Naptime Empires and so she's getting those moms who are balancing everything.

If you have kids and you're listening to this, you definitely know about the struggle of doing it all, like managing the house, managing the children, managing your business.

And so she pokes fun at that and how crazy and... Sorry if I'm about to swear and you need to edit this-

Laura:

That's okay. [laughs]

Bond:

...clusterfucky that whole relationship can be.

I don't recall the copy 100% off the top of my head, but it really plays to that relationship and that role that that person has with their business.

It's a different dynamic that somebody like me, who -- my baby's a dog and doesn't really prevent me from running my business.

For her to speak so in-depth to the mishaps that happen during the day, or the funny things when it comes to prioritizing your family over your business that happen, and just the little things that you can relate to with other moms.

It just gets people clicking because it's like you're not alone.

They feel as if it's a community already, even though it's one person sharing their story and possibly interviewing on a podcast, they feel like they belong in that tribe because they're speaking to that journey.

Laura:

It sounds like really boiling it down to knowing your audience target market so in-depth that you can just speak as if you're speaking to them.

Bond:

Exactly. You know how they always say when you're writing and you write to that one person, you're definitely going to want to do that same thing with your podcast.

You're going to be speaking to that one person who's going through a certain set of challenges, or going through a certain set of successes.

You take that same ideal person and pull that out into all the messaging that you do, getting people to then find out about your podcast and then go over and listen and hopefully become a long-term listener.

Laura:

One thing that I find so refreshing and enjoyable about the emails you send and the copy that you write, is it really sounds like you are writing it.

I feel like I'm talking to you even though I'm not saying anything.

Can you give advice to people about how they can be true and inject their personality? I feel like that is the hard thing for people.

Bond:

It absolutely is and I have to admit when I first started out I always wanted to write like other people. I always wanted to model and emulate people that I thought were being successful.

Then I realized, I would sit there for 30 minutes trying to figure out what the hell is this subject line going to be. It just wasn't productive.

The moment I gave myself permission to be myself and to stop trying to be like other people was the moment that it just started to click and then my email open rates went up and people would respond back saying, just like you said it, "It feels like I'm talking one-to-one."

When I write, I don't filter. I say all the nerdy things that come out of my head, I link off to things that aren't business related just because I think it's a funny joke.

Laura:

That's awesome.

Bond:

It's all about being playful. There's so much focus in this industry in the B2B [Business to Business] and B2C [Business to Consumer] area where people are trying to be serious and focus on conversions and all of the metrics that do matter.

Hell, I'm a strategist. They definitely matter, but it's about the connection.

If you don't have that connection, you're never going to convert them, you're never going to close them, and therefore the relationship never got off the ground in the start.

When I have clients who I'm advising how to move forward with copy for any of their ads, not just podcast related, when they're silly and they're themselves and when they allow themselves to say the things that they truly want to say like ... We were joking the other day about, "Not another podcast where I teach you the seven steps to make 80 gazillion dollars online next week." Right?

Laura:

There's a lot of those.

Bond:

There's a lot of those. If you joke about it and just let that true story and style come through, people will resonate and it's those ads that get clicks. It's those ads that peak curiosity and interest and then allow people to be like, "Damn, if they can be this engaging in a few short sentences, I wonder what they're going to talk about when you have a longer format like a podcast."

We all know with podcasts, it just takes one episode to hook somebody.

Laura:

That's true, that's true. Are you finding any trends, in terms of the length of the copy on the ad, like the box where you type it in, or does it really just depend on the audience and other variations?

Bond:

Yeah, it's the second one. We test absolutely everything and what works for one brand and one audience is going to be completely different than what works for another audience.

There's no formula.

The people that say like, "Here's the Facebook ad formula to get success," I call bullshit on that because it's just truly about being true to yourself and connecting with your audience.

We briefly spoke before about some of the challenges that happen when you're trying to run Facebook ads to podcasts because it's not like a simple LeadPages opt-in. It's not a simple sales funnel, which you just drop your email address and then can be email followed up afterwards.

There are the challenges that you can't necessarily Facebook Pixel people who go off to listen to your podcast because those happen on different platforms.

It's happening in iTunes, it's happening on your phones, it's happening in SoundCloud.

One of the challenges that a lot of people face when running ads is that we're typically leading them to a page that you own, which then pixels them there.

Possibly they go over to iTunes, or you're directing them straight to iTunes and you know there was clicks, but you can't really attribute what happened after those clicks to it when you're looking at the ROI in the data from that.

A few of the things that we try and do and overcome that is really just condition our minds that it's a branding play first and foremost.

Yes, you might not be able to directly measure the exact number of listeners that came from that, but the important metrics that you're going to look like is how many impressions did it get, was it engaging, was there likes and comments and shares on it.

I know those sound like vanity metrics, but brands like Nike invest massive budgets into branding because it's all about just being in front of people all the time with your offerings so that they can build that know, like, and trust factor.

Laura:

Would you say that it's probably smart for people, if they had to choose, if they're running a Facebook ad to actually drive the traffic back to their website where something is embedded there, versus off to an iTunes or some other location?

Bond:

I think it's probably the simplest setup that you can do. If you haven't launched yet, I always recommend that you do send them to a page where it's like, "Find out about my upcoming launch."

If you're doing some pre-marketing, get that email address, get them on a list so that you can own that conversation going forward.

Then you can remind them a few times via email.

But if you're already launched and you're ready to go, even a simple page of "Here's the next steps. Here's what to expect." Once you click this, there's a screenshot you're going to be taken to this page and then you just click here to listen or like a mobile version.

I think that could be really effective because people like familiarity.

If you talk about one thing in your ad and then you talk about the same thing on the page and you send them somewhere, but tell them what to expect, they're more likely to take that action at the end of the day.

Laura:

That's a really good tip too. It's not just the ad and what you have in the ad copy, but what people see once they get off the ad.

You have to have that consistency in wording and images and everything.

Bond:

Absolutely, absolutely.

Laura:

How about on the image? I know from your ADdicted course, which was amazing by the way, plug that ...

Bond:

Thank you. [laughs]

Laura:

[laughs] ...on the image you can only have only so much a percentage of text on the picture. Could you talk a little bit about the text and the image for the ad?

Bond:

Ya! Just because you can put copy on an ad, an image doesn't always mean that you need to.

So, one thing when you're writing copy, you have a few different fields that copy can be entered in.

At the top of your ad you have the main text body, and then you have any copy that you can put on the image itself, and then the headline underneath, as well as the news feed description.

[Here's a blank sample ad below for you to visualize this using a featured image on the shownotes blog for Episode 037[104].]

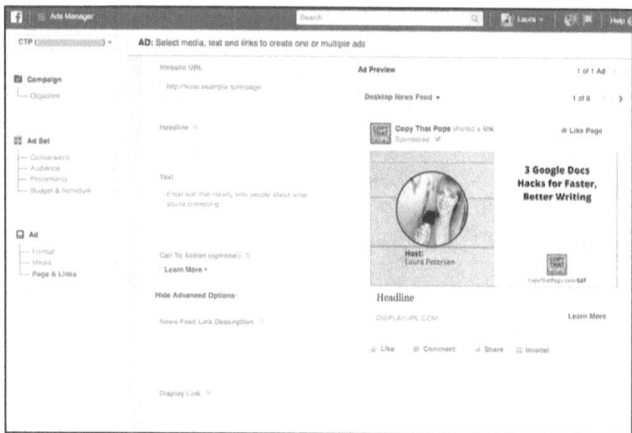

When writing copy I always say to maximize those four spaces by not duplicating things said in the exact same manner.

Don't waste any single character. If you're going to reinforce something, say it in a different way that complements the text above or say it in a different way on your image than you do in the headline.

To answer your question, just because you can put copy on the image doesn't mean you need to. I would always just test.

If you've got really compelling, eye-catching images, you can just lead with an image with no copy on it as well.

---

[104] http://copythatpops.com/037

Laura:

I remember one of the tips you guys talked about in the ADdicted is you want at least your initial interaction with somebody ...you want the ad to almost look like it was shared by a friend. You want it to look very natural.

Bond:

Definitely.

Laura:

Most people aren't necessarily putting text on their images if they're just sharing organically, so worth testing.

Bond:

If it's a shared blog post, whatever the featured image is, it's not always one with text in it. Sometimes it is, but, again, it's a matter of testing.

There's no proven formula that's going to work 100% of the time for absolutely everyone, even though some people out there really want you to believe that.

That's not the case.

Laura:

That's true. I know, I wish I had it. Dang.

Bond:

Yeah, I know. As soon as I find it I'm going to sell it. You can access it for $999.

Laura:

That's a steal. Awesome. Well let's see, anything else that we can think of around copy for podcasters from your experience or clients?

Carousel

Create an ad with 2-10 scrollable images or videos

Bond:

Here's a fun strategy that you can use if you've had some podcasts running for a while and you can figure out which downloads are your most popular.

Use something like a carousel ad to let people select what episode that they would most like to listen to.

If you just took, let's say your 5 top podcasts. And then put them in a carousel, your copy would speak to the 1 thing that they get out of each of those, and then just let them pick which one they want to click to, like a "best of" reel.

Laura:

Wow. I love that. Each image can have its own link off to a different spot?

Bond:

Absolutely.

Laura:

Ohh, I didn't know that. That's a unique way that podcasters could leverage Facebook ads that I hadn't thought of.

Bond:

Yeah, definitely. Even if you have your podcast summary blogs, you could definitely do that as well -

Laura:

Right, the shownotes.

Bond:

- link them to the shownotes via that carousel for your best episodes.

Laura:

That's cool. I love it.

Then I have a bonus question that you could totally skip if you like, but do you get pitched a lot to be interviewed on podcasts?

Bond:

Totally.

Laura:

Then, if so…"yes!" Do you have any dos and don'ts for people on the other end, in terms of how they pitch email you for how they should approach it?

Bond:

I personally just like, even if it's a 1-sentence connection, why their audience would be interested in my message.

Because a lot of the time when your inbox is full and you have requests that aren't very specific on who you're going to be in front of and why that would be a fit, it does get missed. Right?

But if somebody said, "I saw 'this,' which I think would be a great topic to talk about 'here,' is that something you're interested in?" Maybe even an alternative angle that they'd love to talk about.

If you're just blind pitching like, "This is the name of my podcast. We'd love to have you on as a guest." It just doesn't really give enough information to make an educated decision.

Just those little pieces really help to really align with who's the best fit for certain shows.

Laura:

Yeah, it probably makes you, the receiver, feel more special too. They put the time and effort into inviting me for a purpose versus just mass blasting everybody.

Bond:

Absolutely. And if you're pitching yourself for a podcast it's the exact same thing. You want to go to the podcast host and reach out and say, "This is the reason that my message aligns with your audience..."

So know who their audience is. Know what those pain points are that they solve. And then tailor your message to the podcast that you're going to pitch.

Trust me, as somebody who's in this space who gets pitched by podcasts, I am nowhere near what you guys get in terms of people pitching you to be on the podcast.

If you're pitching, you have to be even more specific in standing out in that inbox, because I'm sure there's people ...you know, EOFire gets hundreds a month so to stand out in that field you really just have to be very specific as to what you bring to the table in that interaction.

Laura:

Definitely. That's the common thread really throughout everything with the ads, and the emails, and everything. You need to be super specific and show you've really done your homework to make sure it's the right connection to whomever is receiving it.

Bond:

Yep, absolutely.

Laura:

The theme of the day.

Bond:

The theme of the day is ... I guess you can summarize this whole thing up in that 1 sentence. The connection part is the most important, but the way to connect is to stop making it about you and make it about the audience.

Laura:

Love it.

So many nuggets here in these insights from Amanda to apply to your business. Not only around Facebook ad copy, but also to your emails and messaging, in general!

Thank you, Bond!

PART 3:
REAP YOUR HARVEST

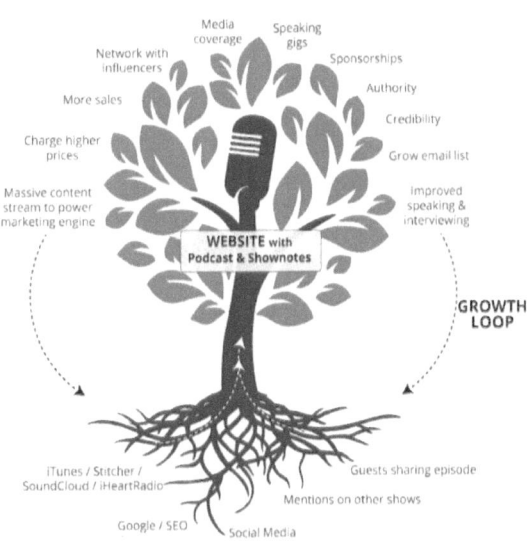

3.1 Conclusion

AS WE SEE FROM the tree image at the beginning of this section, a podcast can be an integral part of a successful business system.

So many benefits are possible for an entrepreneur!

1. Exposure to new audiences
   (e.g. iTunes, Stitcher, SoundCloud, Radio Public iHeartRadio, GooglePlay, Apple CarPlay)

2. Ability to more deeply connect and communicate with your audience

3. Increased credibility

4. Improved industry authority

5. Stronger networking with influencers
   (starting a conversation with "I'd love to put you in front of my audience" sure beats the dreaded "Can I pick your brain over coffee?")

6. Media coverage
   (other podcasts, news articles, T.V., etc.)

7. Lots of great, original content
   (for your inbound marketing efforts)

8. Improved SEO and more web traffic

9. Increased social shares and engagement

10. Email list growth

11. Better speaking and interviewing skills

12. Increased sales of your products and services

13. Ability to charge more for your products and services

14. Sponsorships

15. Paid speaking opportunities

The sky's the limit, really!

It is my sincere hope that if you go through this book, chapter by chapter, you will be able to apply the lessons, examples, and insights from influencers to your own copywriting so that your podcast, brand, and business gets the attention, notoriety, and rewards you deserve.

Remember that writing is the one thing that ties it all together and allows search engines to find you and determine your worthiness for high rankings.

And writing is also among the first things that new visitors see when determining if they want to learn more about your show and business.

If you apply the contents of this book and keep your high-value show consistent, I am confident you will reap all the fruits from the seeds you plant.

To your success,

Laura Petersen

3.2 Acknowledgements

THERE ARE SO MANY people who I have to thank for helping me get this book out into the world and for encouraging me throughout my entrepreneurial journey.

A huge "Thank You!!" to a few biggies:

Devin Shepard

My husband, whose patience, love, and support knows no bounds.

Melissa Sue Tucker

My partner at PodcastTeachers.com and host of Addiction Support Podcast and Minute Meditations (60 Seconds of Solitude).

Dominick Sirianni

My partner at PodtentMarketing.com and the host of IMA Leader.

Brandon T. Adams

Leader of the Influencer Mastermind Accelerator Program[105] that helped spark my drive to write

---

[105] http://livetogrind.com/influencer

this book and hit Best Seller in just 1 month. Creator and Host of Live to Grind, Keys to the Crowd, and Ambitious Adventures.

Emily Hickok

My bestie since Junior High who is an extraordinary lawyer and detail-oriented proofreader. Thank you for editing this book! Your hawk-eyes caught a lot of things to make it clearer.

Olena Beley

We only met last month at the Thrive16 conference and already you have helped me so much. I appreciate your wonderful graphic design work for the front, side, and back of this book!

My Family

My dad (Tim), stepmom (Edith), brother (Adam), and sister-in-law (Isabell) are the best family one could ever ask for.

All the Influencers featured in this book

Thank you for your contributions and sharing your time and knowledge to add extra value to these pages.

All the guests who have come on my podcast Copy That Pops

Your insights and shares have allowed me to grow my own show and reap the benefits we talk about throughout this book. It has been my honor to interview each of you.

Each member of Brandon's Mastermind Accelerator

Thank you for your support and encouragement through the hectic 1-month scramble!

Namely: Dan Tieman, Andria Schultz, and Christina Kalsan.

And: Stephen Dela Cruz, Adrian Aguilar, John Max Bolling, Meghan Alonso, Bernard Paraiso, Sabah Ali, Catherine Howell, Andrea Bergin, Bhomik Saini, Laura Schamberger, Mike Silvestri, Andrew Zalasky, and Gabriel Glynn.

3.3 More Resources

THROUGHOUT THIS BOOK, I have referenced additional tools that could not fit in these pages.

You can grab them all for free here:

www.PodcastTeachers.com/book-freebies

I will continue to add bonuses there as I discover new tools and tricks that can help podcasting entrepreneurs grow their podcast, brand, and business!

Much luck, and ping me on social media with stories of your success.

Facebook: www.facebook.com/LaptopLaura

LinkedIn: www.linkedin.com/in/LauraPetersen

Twitter: www.twitter.com/LaptopLaura

Instagram: www.instagram.com/LaptopLaura

Snapchat: www.snapchat.com/add/LaptopLaura

Index

R

S

T

V

W

Y

Z